THE UNFOLDING OF THE AGES

The
Unfolding of the Ages

Prophecy Fulfilled; Prophecy Being Fulfilled;
Prophecy To Be Fulfilled

by
PAUL R. ALDERMAN, JR.

Introduction by JACOB GARTENHAUS
Foreword by E. SCHUYLER ENGLISH

D. Edmond Hiebert
Collection

LOIZEAUX BROTHERS

Neptune, New Jersey

This testimony for our precious
Saviour is gratefully dedicated
to my beloved wife

JEAN R. ALDERMAN

in sincere appreciation of her
Christlike life, wise counsel
and selfless devotion.

FOREWORD

So much has been spoken and written on Bible prophecy that one would hardly expect to discover an entirely fresh treatment of the subject, yet this is exactly what Mr. Alderman has given us.

Here is a sane, stirring and soul-searching study of the prophetic Word which is, at the same time, invitingly concise. The chapter outlines alone, with their exhaustive lists of Scripture references, are invaluable to the busy reader. Equally important are the appendices which include a splendid resumé of Matthew 24 and 25, a delineation of the noteworthy features of the Revelation, a list of thirty-five Scripture themes that are related to the Second Advent of our Lord, and definitions of thirty-five Bible topics, doctrines and personalities that are associated with the predictive Scriptures.

There will always be, I suppose, some disagreement among Bible students, during this present age, concerning matters that are not wholly vital in the unfolding of future events, as, for example, the specific identity of the two beasts of Revelation 13, or precisely where Ezekiel's Gog and Magog fit into the chronology of the last days. Consequently some may differ with Mr. Alderman on several such items, but they will never find him to be dogmatic in his treatment of these controversial subjects. On the other hand, well-taught evangelicals will be in thorough accord with the author on the essentials of the faith, while untaught readers will learn to divide the Word of truth aright as they consult and ponder this book.

Paul Alderman, the author of two exceedingly helpful volumes, *The Hope That Will Never Fail* and *God's Story of Man's History*, is, like Apollos, "mighty in the Scriptures."

It is a delight to have a share in the publication of this latest work from his pen, to commend him and his ministry to the Lord, and to recommend this book to the Christian public with more than ordinary enthusiasm.

Skytop, Pa.   E. SCHUYLER ENGLISH

INTRODUCTION

I have read with the keenest interest the manuscript, *The Unfolding of the Ages*, and have urged the author to submit it for publication. This work is a collection of studies originally delivered by the author before a group of Christians interested in prophecy, and so great was the enthusiasm with which they received these vital truths that the group grew to a Bible class of some two hundred people.

While recognizing the fact that there are many books on the subject of Bible Prophecy — some of them written in a haphazard manner, others too deep and dry for the average layman — here we have a most fascinating, attractive and comprehensive series of messages in concise form, written by a layman with the keenest insight into Spiritual truths rarely found these days, which will answer the great need of Bible teachers, young ministers and others.

For a number of years I have considered it a privilege to count the author among my most cherished personal friends, and his life has been one of the greatest inspirations to this humble servant. I heartily recommend his volume to all seekers after the truth, and my prayer is that it may enrich the lives of all who read it, as it has enriched my own life.

Atlanta, Ga.   JACOB GARTENHAUS

CONTENTS

PART I

*The Light That Shineth In A
Dark Place: Prophecy Introduced*

Chapter I

BIBLICAL PROPHECY APPRAISED

OUTLINE FOR CHAPTER I

All Scripture is . . . profitable (II Tim. 3:16).

1. Prophecy comprises approximately one-half of the Word of God: Luke 24:25-27; II Pet. 1:21.
2. Prophecy is a prime work of the Holy Spirit: John 16:13; I Tim. 4:1; Rev. 2:7, 11, 17.
3. Prophecy unfolds one of the Word's greatest themes: the glory of Christ: I Pet. 1:11; Rev. 19:10. (See Appendix IV.)
4. Prophecy strengthens faith in God and in His Word: II Pet. 1:19.
5. Prophecy gives light for dark days: Ps. 119:105; II Pet. 1:19.
6. Prophecy protects from false hopes: Matt. 24:4, 25; Matt. 13:36-43; II Tim. 3:1, 13.
7. Prophecy protects from false fears: Matt. 24:4, 25; I Thess. 1:10; I Thess. 5:9; Rev. 3:10.
8. Prophecy gives the right perspective: Rom. 8:18; II Cor. 4:17, 18; II Pet. 3:10-14.
9. Prophecy gives comfort and peace: I Thess. 4:13-18; I Pet. 1:6-8.
10. Prophecy inspires consecration to Christ: Col. 3:4, 5; Titus 2:12-14; I John 3:3; Ps. 119:11.
11. Prophecy inspires self-sacrificial service for Christ: Matt. 24:42-46.
12. Prophecy is understandable: Dan. 9:22, 23, 25; Matt. 24:33; Luke 24:45; II Tim. 3:1; II Pet. 3:3; I John 3:2.

Born with the fateful explosion of an atomic bomb over Hiroshima August 5, 1945, the "Atomic Age" finds a world sinking ever deeper in the throes of unprecedented anxiety, fear and perplexity. There is evident almost universally an atmosphere of crisis, born of both tangible and intangible fears, as the human race gropes feverishly and desperately for an apparently unobtainable solution to the enigma of the hour.

Well indeed might man cry out in the words of Isaiah 21:11, "Watchman, what of the night?" (Literally: "Watchman, what hour of the night?") On the great clock of human history, what, in truth, is the hour? Is midnight truly at hand? Is there only night ahead? Will there be no more glorious and refreshing morningtime of peace and joy and happiness? What saith the Watchman? "The morning cometh, and also the night" (Is. 21:12). The blessed morning is coming indeed, but first the night must become darker. And who vouches for this? None other than almighty God, the Creator and Sovereign of the universe. And by what means is puny, finite man permitted to pierce the veil of the future, and to penetrate the darkness of the unknown? Surely by none other than the message which the infinite God of the universe has graciously given to His sin-wrecked but still beloved creatures: the Word of God, *the Bible*, whose prophetic declarations offer man the *only* possible unveiling of the future. And if ever such light were needed, it is needed desperately today!

That man fails, even refuses, to turn to this one source of desperately needed information during these days of world crisis can only be explained by the deluding power of Satan. Even those who name the name of Christ, and are children of God through faith in His precious, shed blood, are tragically guilty of denying to themselves the precious and powerful message of the sure Word of prophecy, and thus grope in darkness and fear, when they might enjoy the comfort, peace and assurance of its beneficent light.

Although generally denied by man, the fact remains that sin is the great root cause of all the evils and troubles besetting the race today. And, more specifically, it should be noted that "this present evil world (age)" (Gal. 1:4) is running the only course, and fast approaching the only end consistent with the fact that it began with man's rejection and cruel crucifixion of Jesus Christ, the Son of God, who alone is the Prince of Peace. In rejecting Him, man simultaneously chose Satan as the ruler of this age; and, although almighty God over-rules in His never relinquished supremacy, it is nevertheless an inescapable fact that the Devil himself is the god of this age. This is sufficient to explain the character, course and destiny of this present dispensation: it can only be evil; it can only grow worse; and it can end only in judgment.

Thus there are, and must be wars and rumors of wars; there is, and must be "distress of nations, with perplexity"; because Jesus Christ the righteous, Jesus Christ the Prince of Peace, is increasingly ignored by both individuals and nations. The wonder is not that these are indeed perilous times; the wonder is that the grace and love and patience of God have not long been exhausted with a Christ-ignoring, Christ-denying and Christ-rejecting world.

But God made this earth, and created man on it for His pleasure and glory. And while Satan and sin have succeeded in temporarily thwarting the realization of the Divine program earthward, the inescapable fact remains that almighty God is still supreme on His throne as Sovereign of the universe, and will yet, in His time, fully carry out His benign plans on this planet. And He will do this in His way, and through His chosen One: even through the Lord Jesus Christ, His Beloved Son, who alone is worthy to rule as King of kings and Lord of lords.

God has a program; He will carry it out; and He has graciously, for our comfort and guidance, revealed it in great detail in His Word. Thus we approach the sure Word of prophecy in humility, in faith, and in complete dependence upon God the Holy Spirit for guidance and enlightenment.

1. *Prophecy comprises approximately one-half of the Word of God.* It is unthinkable that any part of the Word of God could be unnecessary or superfluous. He is perfect in *all* His ways, and His Word must reflect that divine perfection. *All* Scripture, being the inspired Word of God, must be needful and profitable unto man. To neglect the approximately half of the Word concerned with "things to come" (most of which are yet to be fulfilled) can only result in great Spiritual loss and emaciation for the believer.

2. *Prophecy is a prime work of the Holy Spirit.* Christ, in John 16:13, tells of the coming and work of the Holy Spirit ("the Spirit of truth"): "He will guide you into all truth." And how does Christ say this is to be done? "He will show you things to come." Revelation of prophetic truths is, therefore, one of the prime works of God the Holy Spirit in this age.

3. *Prophecy unfolds one of the Word's greatest themes: the glory of Christ.* In many ways this is the most stupendous of Scriptural doctrines — the coming glorification of the Son of God. It is the burden of the first prophetic message of the Word, Genesis 3:15. Not only is it the major doctrine of the Old Testament, but the 260 New Testament chapters refer to His second coming over 300 times. And it is likewise the burden of the last message from the resurrected and ascended Christ as recorded in Rev. 22.

(See Appendix IV.)

4. *Prophecy strengthens faith in God and in His Word.* The scores and hundreds of Scriptural prophecies which have already been fulfilled exactly and perfectly in every detail not only afford an absolute guarantee of the literal and complete fulfillment of all remaining divine prophecies, but also furnish an inpregnable foundation for an unshakable faith in the God who has spoken these things.

5. *Prophecy gives light for dark days.* These present times are undeniably "dark"; they are nationally and internationally dark; they are dark both politically and economically; they are

especially dark morally and spiritually. Darkness craves light, and the need increases with the deepening of the gloom. As never before, man is groping, desperately needing the light of the prophetic Scriptures.

6. *Prophecy protects from false hopes.* The prophetic Word guards against expecting universal, lasting peace until the Lord Jesus Christ returns to establish it. It protects against expecting universal righteousness while Jesus Christ the righteous is absent. It guards against expecting the world to get better, when it can only get worse and worse, ending in the greatest judgment of all. It guards against expecting the Church to "bring in" and establish Christ's kingdom on earth apart from His personal return to do so. It protects against misconception of the mission of the Church.

7. *Prophecy protects from false fears.* There is no such thing as a sudden catastrophic end of everything; a vague, universal judgment day. To be sure, judgment will fall from God on a Christ-rejecting world, and there is a final day of reckoning when all the wicked dead will stand before the Great White Throne to hear their terrible and eternal verdict: the everlasting Lake of Fire. But God's people are assured protection and deliverance and life eternal; and His Word irrevocably guarantees a new heaven and new earth wherein dwelleth righteousness, once the fires of judgment have burned the last vestige of Satan and sin out of the universe.

8. *Prophecy gives the right perspective.* Being in the flesh, even the Christian is sorely tempted to give undue weight and import to "temporal" things, rather than to things "eternal." The powerful telescope of prophecy brings into real, vivid and thrilling focus the heavenly destiny and blessings of God's children, while, at the same time it causes to pale into their rightful insignificance the things of this brief sojourn on earth.

9. *Prophecy gives comfort and peace.* The Christian is by no means immune to suffering, trial, affliction, tears and bereavement. This is, indeed, in one degree or another, a

"vale of tears" even for the child of God. But, viewed in the light of the prophetic Word, how much do these tribulations lose their sting! There *is* a better day, when God Himself will wipe away all tears from our eyes; when there will be no more sorrow, pain, crying or death; when we *will* be caught up *together* with loved ones (now asleep in Christ) to meet Him in the air and forever be *with Him, and them.* "Wherefore," cries Paul in I Thessalonians 4:18, "comfort one another with these words!"

10. *Prophecy inspires consecration to Christ.* Perhaps the greatest contributing cause to worldliness on the part of Christians is the almost complete neglect of the truths of prophecy. For if the Christian is, in the light of the sure Word of prophecy, constantly awaiting and expecting the return of his Lord from heaven, will not such a believer indeed separate himself from the things of the world so that he will not be found ashamed at the Lord's return? "He that hath this hope in himself, purifieth himself!"

11. *Prophecy inspires self-sacrificial service for Christ.* If the believer knows that the night of judgment fast approaches, will he not be up and about the Master's business of winning precious souls to Christ while it is still the "day of grace"? And, further, if the believer knows from the prophetic Word something of the awfulness of the judgment to come, will he not be all the more burdened to win lost souls to a saving knowledge of the Lamb of God who taketh away the sin of the world? And, if the believer knows that he must stand before the judgment seat of Christ to have his gain or loss of reward determined, will he not the more eagerly "press toward the mark for the prize of the high calling of God in Christ Jesus"?

12. *Prophecy is understandable.* "God is not mocked"; neither does God mock. Would He, the God of love, grace and mercy, offer to unveil the future for us, and then deliberately make the prophetic message beyond our comprehension?

Most assuredly not! The passages cited are sufficient to prove that we are to "know" and "understand" the Word of prophecy. And the great capstone of the Word, THE REVELATION, is precisely that — it is the unveiling of the coming glorification of the Son of God: the climax and consummation of all the prophetic Word. And a special blessing is said (1:3) to await those who read and hear the words of this prophecy.

This is not to say that prophecy will yield its sweet fruits to the casual or careless reader; and certainly not to the one who has not been born-again through the Holy Spirit, for these truths are "spiritually discerned." But for the earnest, humble child of God, who will prayerfully "study to show himself approved unto God, rightly dividing the word of truth," there is God's unfailing promise that the Holy Spirit will indeed show him things to come. But the motive must likewise be proper; God has never promised to reveal His truths just to satisfy idle curiosity, or to fulfill the desires of the one seeking something sensational just for the sake of the sensational. However, when the believer comes to the prophetic Word in humility, prayer and faith, depending entirely on the Holy Spirit, seeking comfort, guidance and inspiration so that he may better serve and increasingly glorify the Lord Jesus Christ in his life, then such a seeker may be sure that he does not come in vain.

CHAPTER II

BIBLICAL PROPHECY DEFINED

1. *The source of prophecy*: The Holy Spirit testifying beforehand. And who, other than God, who alone knows the end from the beginning, can testify beforehand? Man guesses, but never testifies with assurance as to what the morrow may bring. As one has well said: "We might as soon think to pluck the stars from heaven as to wrest its secrets from the future. We cannot foresee even dimly the events of tomorrow, or of the next hour. We (in our own foresight) stand before a wall of impenetrable darkness." "But there is a God in heaven that maketh known what shall be."

2. *The subject of prophecy.* Perhaps more than any other single thing, this must be grasped: THE LORD JESUS CHRIST IS THE SUBECT OF BIBLICAL PROPHECY. Many and varied are the secondary subjects of Scriptural Prophecy, but their one purpose, their one justification for being a part of the divine Word is that they have as their ultimate object and theme, THE LORD JESUS CHRIST. Christ, the Word of life, and the Bible, the Word of truth, are absolutely inseparable. Thus it is, and must be, that any profitable and edifying study of the prophetic Word must have the Lord Jesus Christ as object, center and goal; otherwise the way is wide open for unspeakable misunderstanding, confusion and error.

3. *The scope of prophecy.* What is prophecy? The Holy Spirit testifying beforehand. Of whom does He prophetically testify? THE LORD JESUS CHRIST. What does He testify concerning Christ? (1) The *sufferings* of Christ and (2) the *glory* which should follow. The nutshell of all prophecy, Genesis 3:15, confirms this; for in that seed-germ of the prophetic Word, God foretold both the sufferings (Satan shall bruise His heel), and the glory to follow (Christ shall bruise his head).

Very often these two themes were not clearly distinguished in the Old Testament prophecies, because the interval of the present age was unrevealed then. Thus, for example, in Isaiah 61:1, 2, the sufferings and the glory are separated only by a comma in the second verse. In quoting this passage (Luke 4:18, 19) Christ gave a vivid illustration of the incalculable importance of "rightly dividing the word of truth"; for He read no further than "the acceptable year of the Lord," thus signifying that His first advent was "to suffer many things" in order that, through His shed blood, the saving grace of God might be proclaimed to all men everywhere in this "the acceptable year of the Lord." But as surely as He suffered, so will He yet be glorified on this very earth that witnessed the greatest of all crimes, for He will yet proclaim "the day of vengeance of our God."

Living as we do, in the age of grace, between the Cross (sufferings) and the Crown (glory), "we have the word of prophecy made more sure" as we examine the unfulfilled prophecies relating to His glorification in the light of the perfectly fulfilled prophecies relating to His sufferings.

BIBLICAL PROPHECY UNLOCKED

OUTLINE FOR CHAPTER III

Open thou mine eyes, that I may behold wondrous things out of thy law (Ps. 119:18).

Key 1: Regeneration through the Word of God: John 3:3-8; John 16:13; I Cor. 2:14.

Key 2: Rightly using the Word of God: I Cor. 2:9-13; II Pet. 1:20.

Key 3: Rightly dividing the Word of God: II Tim. 2:15.

    a. Israel and the Church: to be distinguished as to: (1) *Calling* (Gen. 12:1-3 and Deut. 8:7-9 with Phil. 3:20, Heb. 3:1 and I Pet. 1:4); (2) *Conduct* (Ex. 21:23-25 and Deut. 7:1, 2 with I Cor. 4:11-13); and (3) *Destiny* (Is. 11:11, 12; 14:1 and Jer. 16:14, 15; 23:5, 6 with John 14:1-3 and Phil. 3:20, 21 and I Thess. 4:13-18).

    b. Christ's First Advent and Second Advent: Is. 53 and Luke 2:6, 7 with Dan. 7:13, 14 and Matt. 24:30.
        (1) First: the Lamb of God — the sufferings, the Cross.
        (2) Second: the Lion of the Tribe of Judah — the glory, the Crown.

    c. The two phases of Christ's return: I Thess. 4:13-18, Titus 2:13a with Titus 2:13b and Rev. 19:11-16.
        (1) "The blessed hope": He comes secretly, in the air, to the Church, as the Bridegroom for His Bride, to a marriage, as the Morning Star, *before* the Tribulation.
        (2) "The glorious appearing": He comes publicly, to the earth, to Israel, as the King of kings, to a judgment, as the Sun of Righteousness, *after* the Tribulation.

    d. The Judgments:
        (1) "The Judgment Seat of Christ" (II Cor. 5:10). *Time and Place*: I Cor. 4:5 and I Thess. 4:17. *Subjects*:

Rom. 14:10 and II Cor. 5:9, 10. *Basis*: I Cor. 3:11-13. *Results*: I Cor. 3:14, 15.

(2) "The Throne of His Glory" (Matt. 25:31). *Time and Place*: Matt. 25:31. *Subjects*: Matt. 25:32. *Basis*: Matt. 25:40 and 45. *Results*: Matt. 25:46.

(3) "The Great White Throne" (Rev. 20:11). *Time and Place*: Rev. 20:11. *Subjects*: Rev. 20:12. *Basis*: Rev. 20:12 and 13. *Results*: Rev. 20:14 and 15.

e. The Resurrections: John 5:29.

(1) The First: the redeemed — *before* the Millennium, unto life eternal (I Cor. 15 and Rev. 20:4-6).

(2) The Second: the lost — *after* the Millennium, unto death eternal (Rev. 20:5, 11-15).

Note: See Appendix I, Definitions 1, 2, 7, 14, 16, 17, 18, 19, 29, 30, 31, 33.

Are there keys available to open the doors of the prophetic Scriptures so that we may, with understanding, assurance and blessing enter into the priceless treasures of an unveiled future? To be sure there are; for the Bible is God's message to man, given through men, and in the language of man, that mankind might have a complete and understandable revelation from his Maker. Of the means which God has given for the understanding of the prophetic Scriptures, we shall briefly consider three which are undeniably essential and fundamental, although by no means the only ones:

Key 1: Regeneration through the Word of God. If, as is certainly true, it is impossible for the natural man to receive "the things of the Spirit of God because they are spiritually discerned," it is more than obvious that unregenerate man cannot hope to enter into God's secrets of the future. These things of the future are revealed only through God the Holy Spirit; and man without Christ, man who has never been born again, man who is still dead in trespasses and sins cannot possibly hope to enter into the "family secrets" of prophecy.

Key 2: Rightly using the Word of God. The Holy Spirit is the Revealer of "things to come," and the Word of God is the mode of revelation. There is one Author (the Holy Spirit) and one Theme (the Lord Jesus Christ) and one Word (the Bible), so there must be perfection, unity and harmony as the message of prophecy is unfolded through the Holy Scriptures. And just as Scripture perfectly harmonizes with Scripture, so does a comparison of Scripture with Scripture wonderfully afford the means by which the prophetic Word interprets itself. As word is compared with word, verse with verse, passage with passage, book with book, Old Testament with New Testament, the Word of prophecy clearly and wonderfully yields its precious treasures to the sincere, believing and earnest child of God. This is by no means to exclude the invaluable help obtainable from men of God into whose labors we are permitted to enter, but, in the final analysis, the Word itself must be its own interpreter.

Key 3: Rightly dividing the Word of God. The Christian must *study* to show himself approved unto God, a workman that needeth not to be ashamed (II Tim. 2:15). And how shall he study? What course shall he follow as he compares Scripture with Scripture? The answer is clear and vital: "Rightly dividing the word of truth." The perfect Word of a perfect God must be perfect in all its order, arrangement and divisions, and so it is. And if the divine arrangement and divisions are not respected, if the divine Word is not "rightly divided," only confusion and misunderstanding can result.

The accompanying outline briefly lists some of the great themes and subjects of the Word of prophecy which *must* be handled aright and properly distinguished if they are to be grasped. A glance is sufficient to indicate the immeasurable confusion and loss which would result if there were a failure to divide the Word rightly as these subjects are studied.

In conclusion, we shall do well to heed the words of Dr. C. I. Scofield on this important subject: "The Word of Truth, then, has right divisions, and it must be evident that, as one cannot be 'a workman that needeth not to be ashamed' without observing them, so *any study* of that Word which ignores those divisions must be in large measure profitless and confusing."

CHAPTER IV

BIBLICAL PROPHECY SUMMARIZED

Seventy ["sevens" of years] are determined . . . to seal up the . . . prophecy (Dan. 9:24-27).

1. God's program: Dan. 9:24.
    a. "To make reconciliation for iniquity": The Sufferings of Christ. — (The present interval)
    b. "To bring in everlasting righteousness": The Glory of Christ.
2. God's timetable: Dan. 9:25, 27. From the going forth of the commandment to restore and build Jerusalem, unto the consummation, seventy "sevens" of years determined:
    a. Seven "sevens" (49 years) to rebuilding of Jerusalem, "even in troublous times," by Nehemiah and Ezra.
    b. And sixty-two 'sevens' (434 years) to Messiah the Prince, Christ's First Advent: John 1:11; Gal. 4:4. — (The present interval)
    c. And one 'seven' (7 years), to the consummation:
        (1) He (Antichrist) confirms covenant (treaty) with the many (majority of Israel) for (this) one "seven" (of years).
        (2) He causes the sacrifice and oblation to cease (breaks covenant) in midst of the "seven" (of years).
        (3) Because of the overspreading of abominations (desecration of the Holy temple and sacrifices in Jerusalem by Antichrist), wars and *desolations* (the great unprecedented Tribulation) are determined *until the consummation* (the end) when that determined shall be poured upon the desolator (doom of Antichrist).
3. The present interval: Dan. 9:26. *After* the sixty-two "sevens" (of years).
    a. Messiah cut off (crucified) and had nothing (denied that which rightly belonged to Him).

25

b. The city (Jerusalem) and sanctuary (Temple) destroyed by the people (Romans) of the prince that shall come (Antichrist); this end (of the city and temple) coming with a flood (indescribable bloodshed) (70 A.D.).

c. Wars and desolations determined unto the end (seven-year *consummation* of the age). (Thus described is the course of this interval, this present age, between the Cross and the Crown.)

Note: See Appendix I, Definition 8.

We come now to get a "bird's eye" view of prophecy, a grasp of its theme as a whole, so that there may be an understanding of the details as they unfold, and so that there may be a proper and understandable inter-relation of the various parts to each other and to the whole.

The background to Daniel 9:24-27 is vital, so a brief word is in order. The scene is in Babylon, then ruler of the world. The time is about 538 B.C. The man is Daniel, the aged and beloved prophet of the Lord, who had been carried captive as a youth by Nebuchadnezzar when God gave Jerusalem and the Jews into his hands because of their continued disobedience. Daniel had been reading the Word of God and the Holy Spirit has directed his attention to the prophecy of Jeremiah (25:11,12), which foretold that the Babylonian captivity would last for seventy years. Daniel realizes these seventy years are about expired, and he begins to pour out his heart to God in prayer on behalf of his beloved people, confessing their sins, and pleading with the Lord to forgive His people and restore them to the Promised Land.

In the midst of his prayer, Gabriel the great angel, arrives with an answer from God, and this message, as recorded in verses 24-27, not only tells Daniel what is going to happen in the immediate future to his people, Israel, and to the Promised Land, but goes on to the time of the end when God will have, through Christ, overthrown Satan and sin and brought in everlasting righteousness.

Since this is essentially a great "time prophecy," it is

necessary to know what is meant by the "seventy weeks," and exactly when they began to run their course.

First, let it be noted that the word "weeks" literally means "sevens"; so the prophecy says "seventy sevens" are determined to accomplish God's whole purpose earthward. That this means "sevens" of *years*, and not of any other period, is beyond controversy. The context proves it, because Daniel was thinking and praying in terms of the seventy-year Babylonian captivity; and now God tells him that seven times seventy years are allotted for His whole program earthward. Further, a reference to Genesis 29:27 and Leviticus 25:8 will confirm this as the correct interpretation. And, finally, history, as it has faithfully recorded the exact and precise fulfillment, at exactly the right time, of the fulfilled portion of this prophecy, places the seal of certainty on interpreting these "sevens" (or "weeks") as years.

And what is the starting point of these 490 years? Verse twenty-five clearly identifies this with "the going forth of the commandment to restore and to build Jerusalem." Nehemiah 2:1-8 records this commandment as it was given by Artaxerxes, the Persian monarch, to Nehemiah, a Jew and cupbearer to the king. From this date, the 490 years are to run their course, divided into three unequal periods: 49 years, 434 years, and 7 years. The first two periods have run their course, or a total of 483 years which, as foretold, ended precisely with the final and official rejection of the Messiah, to be followed a few days later by His being "cut off" (crucified). And this tragedy of all tragedies stopped God's prophetic clock, leaving 7 years of the 490 yet to run.

Verse twenty-five describes in a threefold manner this interval between the 483 years and the last 7, and this description shows conclusively that this present interval is of indefinite duration. After the 483 years expired (with Christ's official offering of Himself as the Messiah and His official rejection by Israel during the Last Week) the following has taken place as prophesied: (1) Messiah was "cut-off" (crucified) shortly thereafter; (2) Jerusalem was destroyed and the temple also in 70 A.D. by the Romans, and (3) wars and desolations continue to characterize the course of this age which began with Calvary and ends with His return in glory.

To briefly recapitulate:

1. *God's Program*: To bring in, ultimately, everlasting righteousness on this earth by overthrowing, through Christ, Satan and sin.

    a. To make reconciliation for iniquity, there must first have been "the sufferings of Christ," because "without shedding of blood is no remission of sin."

    b. Then comes the "glory to follow," when Christ will bring in everlasting righteousness and peace at His personal, visible, triumphant return.

2. *God's Timetable*: A total of 490 years for carrying out His earthward program through Israel.

    a. During the first forty-nine years (from commandment of Artaxerxes to Nehemiah) Jerusalem was rebuilt. This was literally and exactly carried out by Ezra, Nehemiah and the other faithful ones; the walls were finished in a few months, but the city and temple not until the forty-nine years were expired.

    b. The basic reason for this restoration of a remnant to Palestine was to prepare for the coming of the Christ (through Israel, according to the flesh). He came, offered Himself as the promised Messiah, was rejected and crucified exactly *when* and how it had been predicted: at the end of the 434 years.

    c. Following the crucifixion, God stopped the prophetic clock, leaving seven years yet to run. During this interval, Israel is scattered among the nations, and God is calling out a people for His name—the Church. Since these last seven years will be a time of unprecedented judgment and anguish for a

Christ-rejecting world just preceding the glorious return of the King of kings, He has promised to come for His Bride, the Church, before wrath strikes (Rev. 3:10). Further, He has foretold the re-gathering of Israel to her land preparatory to His carrying out, through them, His predicted program for the whole earth. Thus, as this present evil age runs its course, and the awful seven-year Tribulation draws nigh, the days grow more evil and perilous, Israel begins to return to Palestine, and the Church (born-again believers) awaits that blessed hope when it shall in a moment be caught up to be delivered from the wrath to come (I Thess. 4:13-18 and II Thess. 5:9) — the terrible wrath of a holy and righteous God against a world grown so wicked it will be ruled by the Antichrist in person during those final seven years.

3. *The Present Interval*: It is the age of grace, by virtue of the great love of God which has turned man's greatest crime into his opportunity for salvation, through man's believing on the Christ who was slain for our sins, and who arose for our justification. But the basic nature of this interval must be clearly kept in mind if the Word is to be rightly divided: This age lies in the power of Satan (as man rejected Christ), is increasingly evil, and faces certain judgment when the final seven years of Daniel's great prophecy run their predicted course. It is, therefore, only to be expected that there will be wars and rumors of wars and desolations and evils of all kinds, until Jesus Christ the righteous, the Prince of Peace, returns to take over the government of the world.

CHAPTER V

BIBLICAL PROPHECY CERTIFIED BY GOD

30

3. Prophecy certified by the word of God: Is. 45:23.
   a. His Word is true: Ps. 119:160; John 17:17.
   b. His Word is unchangeable: I Sam. 15:29; Matt. 5:18.
   c. His Word is everlasting: Ps. 117; 119:89; Is. 40:8; I Pet. 1:24, 25.
   d. His Word is irresistible: Is. 55:11.

1. *Prophecy certified by the nature of God.* Finite man cannot possibly fully know and understand the infinite Creator and Sovereign of the universe. Perhaps the name by which He declared Himself to Moses, "I am that I am," comes as near summarizing His divine attributes as any one title could. It is He, the Almighty One, who has spoken the Word of prophecy, declaring the end from the beginning, because to Him there is only one eternal present. Therefore we indeed have the "Word of prophecy made more sure" because it all rests upon an irresistible "Thus saith the Lord."

2. *Prophecy certified by the character of God.* His faithfulness to the living Word, and to the written Word demands that every detail of prophecy be exactly fulfilled. His challenged glory and honour join His outraged holiness and righteousness in demanding that as He has spoken so shall it come to pass. His perfect justice toward the wicked and His sweet mercy toward the persecuted child of God unite in crying out for prophecy's fulfillment. And He changes not; His immutability undergirds all the prophetic Word with a divine guarantee that is unshakable.

3. *Prophecy certified by the Word of God.* The Word of Him who is the Truth, must be true in an absolute and perfect sense. Whether that Word concerns things past, present or in the far-off future, its absolute truthfulness remains a certain fact. Likewise, it is unchangeable, eternal and irresistible. Having all knowledge, power and wisdom when He uttered the Word of Prophecy, it is inconceivable that anything could ever happen to warrant any change in it. Every-

thing and all of time was perfectly known to Him when He spoke the Word. Therefore it is everlasting because it transcends time and all things temporal. And His Word is irresistible. It could not be otherwise, being absolute Truth, unchangeable Truth, and eternal Truth.

CHAPTER VI

BIBLICAL PROPHECY CERTIFIED BY GOD'S RECORD

   b. Edom (Esau), Israel's implacable enemy: Ezek. 35:1-15;
      Obad. 18.
      (1) Land laid desolate, as prophesied.
      (2) Cities destroyed, never to be rebuilt, as prophesied.
      (3) People extinct, as prophesied.
   c. Cyrus, Persian Monarch.
      (1) Foretold by name and mission: Is. 44:28; 45:1-4;
          Jer. 29:10.
      (2) Fulfilled nearly two centuries later: Ezra 1:1-4.
   d. Rebuilder of Jericho.
      (1) His oldest and youngest sons to die during its recon-
          struction: Josh. 6:26.
      (2) Fulfilled approximately five hundred years later: I Kings
          16:34.
   e. The universal flood.
      (1) Predicted: Gen. 6:17.
      (2) Fulfilled: Gen. 7:17-24.
      "We have the [unfulfilled] word of prophecy
          made more sure" (II Pet. 1:19).
Note: See Appendix I, Definition 13.

Not only is the prophetic Word certified and guaranteed
by God's nature, God's character and God's Word, but the
portions yet unfilled are further underwritten by the inescapable fact of prophecy fulfilled. Whether the prophecy concerns
a minor matter, or a world empire; whether it was uttered days,
decades, centuries or millenniums prior to fulfillment; whether
it is fulfilled suddenly or progressively; whether it is accomplished through human instrumentality, or directly by divine
action; regardless of these, or any other factors, God's prophetic
record is perfect.

1. *As concerning Israel, He spake and it was done.* It is
interesting to note that these prophecies in Leviticus and
Deuteronomy were uttered even before Israel entered the
Promised Land from Egypt.

2. *As concerning the Gentile nations, He spake and it was
done.* Through Daniel, about 600 B.C., God said that, until
the establishment of Christ's kingdom on earth at His return,

there would be four (no more or less) Gentile world powers. There have been these four, and no others. Babylon was first, followed by Media-Persia, then Greece, and finally Rome, as predicted. No nation has held world-wide sway since Rome, and none will until Rome is revived for a brief season as prophesied, at the end of the age, to feel the well-merited judgment-wrath of God for the role she played in the death of His Beloved Son at Calvary.

3. *As concerning divers and sundry things, He spake and it was done.* Just a glance at the five prophecies here cited will show that they all have one thing in common: from a human standpoint, each would have appeared improbable, if not impossible, of fulfillment. Would Tyre, proud and unchallenged mistress of the sea indeed fall, and fall so terribly that she would become only a rubbish pile on which the fishers would spread their nets? But so it happened. First, she felt the blows of Nebuchadnezzar of Babylon, and then over two centuries later, Alexander the Great completed her destruction and desolation exactly as foretold by Ezekiel. Likewise Esau, although apparently secure in her impregnable mountain fortress, went down under the irresistible force of the Word of prophecy. Cyrus, proud Persian monarch, was but a pliable tool in the hand of God as he precisely fulfilled a two-hundred-year-old prophecy. Hiel, the Bethelite, evidently did not believe the prophetic Word, or else he must have had little love for his sons; for he brought on their untimely death, as predicted by Joshua five hundred years previously, when he rebuilt accursed Jericho.

And what of the universal flood? Except for eight souls, the human race laughed in the face of God when He predicted such a catastrophe. How, thought they (in their feigned wisdom), could such a thing happen? It had never happened before. But the sure Word of prophecy had been uttered by almighty God, and the Flood became history, tragic history.

In concluding our meditations on prophecy fulfilled, we

briefly consider a series of most remarkable predictions concerning *Egypt,* which although a relatively insignificant nation today, was at one time a mighty world power in every sense of the word. Isaiah 19:1-15 and Ezekiel 29 and 30 afford the basis for these observations. Isaiah spoke about 700 B.C. and Ezekiel about 600 B.C., at which time Egypt was a mighty power and, in a sense, "Queen of the Nations." And though her downfall seemed most unlikely, and though it came gradually over a period of ten or twelve centuries, history has faithfully recorded an exact and complete fulfillment of the prophetic Word concerning this ancient enemy of Israel. Beginning with Nebuchadnezzar about 600 B.C. and continuing until the invasion by the Mohammedan hordes about 600 A.D., here is how God prophesied He would bring this haughty nation low:

Her ancient and glorious capitals to be desolated.

Her rivers and canals to be dried up.

Papyrus reeds, and other wealth-producing verdure swept away.

Fisheries and other industries to fail.

Land to decay, and be desolate. Surrounding countries to be desolate.

Her masters to be wicked and cruel strangers ("foreigners").

Her masters to waste her land.

Her existence to continue in her land, but as the basest kingdom.

No native son to sit on her throne. (None has since 350 B.C.)

PART II
The Sufferings of Christ:
Prophecy Fulfilled

CHAPTER VII

HIS LINEAGE, BIRTH AND LIFE

OUTLINE FOR CHAPTER VII

He made himself of no reputation, and took upon him the form of a servant, and was made in the likeness of men (Phil. 2:7).

1. His lineage: Gen. 3:15.
   a. The Seed of Shem: Gen. 9:26.
   b. The Seed of Abraham: Gen. 12:3.
   c. The Seed of Isaac: Gen. 17:19.
   d. The Seed of Jacob: Gen. 28:14.
   e. The Seed of Judah: Gen. 49:10.
   f. The Seed of David: II Sam. 7:16.
   g. The Seed of the Virgin: Is. 7:14.
      Fulfillment: Matt. 1:1-17 and Luke 3:23-38.
2. His birth: Gal. 4:4, 5.
   a. The manner: Is. 7:14 and Luke 1:26-31.
   b. The place: Mic. 5:2 and Luke 2:1-7.
   c. The forerunner: Is. 40:3 and Matt. 3:1-3.
3. His life: Is. 42:1; Mark 10:45.
   a. "Full of grace": Is. 61:1, 2a; Luke 7:19-22; John 1:14.
   b. "Unwanted": Is. 53:2 and Matt. 8:34; 13:57; Luke 9:58; John 1:11; 5:40.
   c. "Despised and rejected": Is. 53:3 and Matt. 12:14; Mark 3:21; John 18:39, 40; 19:14, 15; Acts 3:13-15.
   d. "Acquainted with grief": Is. 53:4a and John 11:35-38; Heb. 4:15.

Note: See Appendix I, Definitions 1 and 33.

37

"First he must suffer many things, and then enter into his glory." His sufferings were made inescapable by the sure Word of prophecy. "All things must be fulfilled, which were written in the law of Moses, and in the Prophets, and in the Psalms, concerning me." Thus did the Lord Jesus Christ set His seal upon all the Old Testament (in its threefold division), and especially upon the more than three hundred specific prophecies relating to His first advent, when He came to give His life a ransom for our souls.

1. *His lineage*. God had promised Abraham (Gen. 12:3) that in his seed all the families of the earth would be blessed. And God had promised David that his seed would one day establish the Davidic throne forever. Thus Matthew, whose record is the Gospel of the King, traces Christ's genealogy back to both Abraham and David. On the other hand, Luke, writing the Gospel of the Son of Man, quite naturally traces Christ's genealogy back to Adam, proving that He is the promised seed of the woman (Gen. 3:15). Thus fully and perfectly did Jesus of Nazareth identify Himself, by His lineage, as the promised Messiah.

It is more than interesting to note that this particular line of prophecy began about 4,000 B.C. (Gen. 3:15) and ran to about 750 B.C. (Is. 7:14). The passing of millenniums only served to add emphasis to the Messiahship of Jesus of Nazareth.

2. *His birth*. "In the fulness of time, God sent forth his Son." At precisely the right moment He came; at exactly the time that would cause His rejection and crucifixion to be just at the time foretold by Daniel centuries before (Dan. 9:24-27). And He was born of a Virgin, just as predicted. And in Bethlehem, just as predicted, although to accomplish this seemingly impossible fulfillment of Micah's prophecy (5:2), God had to move the proud Roman Emperor, Caesar Augustus, to issue a decree of taxation which caused Joseph to take Mary to Bethlehem just at that time. And He was pre-

ceded by the forerunner, John the Baptist, as predicted by Isaiah.

3. *His life.* He, alone, ever fully did the will of God (Ps. 40:8); and He, alone, did only good to man, so that "they wondered at the gracious words which proceeded out of his mouth." He came, "full of grace and truth," tirelessly ministering to all of the manifold needs of mankind. Even His enemies admitted His complete innocency and purity of life, and had to say, "Never man spake like this man." But He was despised, and rejected; unwanted and shunned! "He came unto his own and his own received him not," just as God had foretold.

Chapter VIII

HIS SUFFERINGS AND DEATH

Outline for Chapter VIII

He . . . became obedient unto death, even the death of the cross (Phil. 2:8).

1. Gethsemane: Is. 53:3 and Matt. 26:36-38.
   a. Assailed by Satan: Gen. 3:15 and John 14:30.
   b. Betrayed by His familiar friend: Ps. 41:9; Zech. 11:12, 13 and Matt. 26:14-16, 47-50.
   c. Arrested by His enemies and forsaken by His disciples: Zech. 13:7 and Matt. 26:31, 50, 56.
2. Gabbatha: Dan. 9:26 and Matt. 26:63-66.
   a. Falsely accused: Ps. 109:2, 3 and Matt. 26:59-61.
   b. Silent before accusers: Is. 53:7 and Matt. 27:12-14.
   c. Smitten: Mic. 5:1 and Matt. 27:30.
   d. Spit Upon: Is. 50:6 and Matt. 26:67.
   e. Mocked: Ps. 69:12 and Luke 22:63-65.
   f. Scourged: Ps. 129:3; Is. 53:5 and John 19:1.
   g. Unjustly condemned: Is. 53:8 and Matt. 27:3, 4, 22-24.
3. Golgotha: Ps. 22:16 and Luke 23:33.
   a. Numbered with transgressors: Is. 53:12 and Mark 15:27, 28.
   b. Hands and feet pierced (crucified): Ps. 22:14-17 and Luke 23:33.
   c. Gall to drink: Ps. 69:21 and Matt. 27:33, 34.
   d. Scorned and derided: Ps. 22:6-8 and Matt. 27:39-44.
   e. Garments parted: Ps. 22:18 and John 19:23, 24.
   f. Intercession for persecutors: Is. 53:12b and Luke 23:34.
   g. Forsaken of God: Ps. 22:1; Is. 53:4, 10 and Matt. 27:46.
   h. Death: Ps. 22:15 and Luke 23:46; John 19:30.
   i. Bones unbroken: Ps. 34:20 and John 19:32, 33, 36.
   j. Side pierced: Zech. 12:10 and John 19:34, 37.
   k. Buried: Is. 53:9 and Matt. 27:57-60.

1. For our transgressions: Is. 53:5, 6, 11 and II Cor. 5:21; I Pet. 2:24.

Note: See Appendix I, Definitions 1 and 33.

1. *Gethsemane.* Not in this life will any mortal man fathom Gethsemane. There had to be far more than physical fear of death; far more even than any mental agony; there was a sorrow that struck down the Son of God, an indescribable burden that caused Him to cry out in anguish for the Father to remove the cup if possible, if it could be according to His will. But the cup must be drunk; the sin question must be settled once-for-all; and there was one way, and one alone — the Lamb of God must shed His precious blood on Calvary. He, the Sinless One, must be made sin for us; He, the Holy One, must bear our sins; He, the Innocent One, must feel our guilt. The betrayal by His erstwhile disciple, Judas; the arrest by the cruel mob; the grief and pain of being forsaken at such a time by all His disciples; all these were the lot of the Man of Sorrows. But surely it was His combat unto the death with Satan and sin that broke His heart and caused His unspeakable agony.

2. *Gabbatha.* Just as Gethsemane (garden of the "oil-presses") witnessed the sweat of blood from the Man of Sorrows, so does Gabbatha (the "Pavement") fittingly become the scene of His sufferings at the hands of men whose hearts were no less hard than the stones upon which they stood. Never was satanic hatred more viciously vented upon man than when the falsely accused Creator was dragged into the place of judgment by His sin-hardened creatures to be smitten, spit upon, derided and cruelly scourged, and, finally, condemned unjustly to death by admittedly lying witnesses. But His great heart of love yearned for the salvation of even such sinners, and so he "who did no sin, neither was guile found in his mouth" was silent before His accusers and "when he was reviled, reviled not again" (I Pet. 2:22, 23).

3. *Golgotha.* And where, but "the place of a skull" (Gol-

gotha) would the Son of God come to final grips with that last great enemy, Death? And how would he die? By crucifixion, exactly as foretold by David in Psalm 22 hundreds of years before the cruel Romans invented this mode of death for the basest of criminals. The accompanying outline embodies a sufficient number of the detailed prophecies as to just how He would die to prove marvelously again that the sure Word of prophecy always has its perfect fulfillment. And if the blessed Saviour felt that wrath of Satan in a peculiar way in Gethsemane, and the anger of man in all its fierceness at Gabbatha, then surely at Golgotha His cup of suffering was filled to overflowing when He felt the fury of a holy God against sin.

Finally, when the debt of sin had been fully settled, and when every minute prophecy concerning His sufferings and death were perfectly fulfilled, He cried, "It is finished" and He gave up the ghost.

"He humbled himself, and became obedient unto death, even the death of the cross. Wherefore God also hath highly exalted him, and given him a name which is above every name: that at the name of Jesus every knee should bow . . . and that every tongue should confess that Jesus Christ is Lord" (Phil. 2:8-11).

PART III
The Glory Which Shall Follow:
Prophecy To Be Fulfilled

CHAPTER IX

THE CERTAINTY OF HIS GLORIFICATION

OUTLINE FOR CHAPTER IX
The stone which the builders refused is become the head stone of the corner (Ps. 118:22).
1. Assured by His resurrection: Acts 17:31.
2. Pledged by God the Father: Ps. 2:6-9; Ps. 16:10 and Acts 2:30, 31; Ps. 110:1; Is. 53:12; Dan. 7:13, 14; Mic. 5:15; Rev. 5:1-12.
3. Predicted by God the Son: Matt. 19:28; 24:27-30; 26:64; John 14:1-3; Rev. 22:7, 12, 20.
4. Promised by God the Holy Spirit: I Pet. 1:11.
5. Affirmed by the holy angels: Acts 1:10, 11.
6. Declared by the inspired servants of God: Gen. 3:15; II Sam. 7:16; Ps. 24:1-10; Is. 11:10-12; Jer. 23:5, 6; Dan. 7:13, 14; Hos. 3:4, 5; Mic. 4:7; Zech. 2:10-12; Matt. 24:27-30; Mark 13:24-27; Luke 21:25-27; John 14:2, 3; Acts 1:11; Rom. 11:25, 26; Col. 3:4; II Thess. 2:7, 8; Titus 2:13; Heb. 9:28; Jude 14, 15; Rev. 19:11-16; II Pet. 1:21.
7. Guaranteed by fulfilled prophecy: II Pet. 1:19.
Note: See Appendix I, Definitions 2, 10 and 14.

The widespread neglect, on the part of the Lord's people, of the greatest theme of the Word, the glorification of the Lord Jesus Christ, is as tragic as it is inconceivable. As is indicated in Appendix IV, this is *the* central subject of the Holy Word of God; it is the goal toward which all else flows; the logical,

43

righteous and avowed consummation of God's plans and purposes earthward. He humbled Himself, even unto death, *wherefore* God also hath highly exalted Him. What an all-important and powerful word is that "wherefore"! It says that because He suffered, He must be glorified; it says that, however much He suffered, the more must He be glorified; it says that because He perfectly fulfilled the first portion of the Word of prophecy (The Sufferings), He must and will perfectly fulfill the second portion (The Glory).

Among others, the outline lists seven absolutely certain guarantees of His glorification:

1. *It is assured by His resurrection.* God hath literally and unequivocably "given assurance unto all men" of the coming glorification of His Son in that He hath raised Him from the dead. That He lives is "the best established fact in history"; and He lives to *reign.*

2. *It is pledged by God the Father.* "Shall not the Judge of all the earth do right?" Will He not avenge His Beloved Son of the greatest crime of the ages? What saith the Word of prophecy? "God hath sworn with an oath that he would raise up Christ to sit on his throne." "And God is not man that he should lie; neither the son of man that he should repent [change]: hath he said, and shall he not do it? or hath he spoken, and shall he not make it good?"

3. *It is predicted by God the Son.* When on earth, Christ spoke little of His first advent, but much of His coming glory. And He who is the Truth cannot lie.

4. *It is promised by God the Holy Spirit.* The ministry of the Holy Spirit is not to speak of Himself, but to show forth the things of Christ; and foremost in His work is the declaration of "things to come," of which the central theme is the coming glorification of the Son. The Holy Spirit testified of His sufferings, *and* the glory which should follow.

5. *It is affirmed by the Holy angels.* They truthfully heralded His first coming, and, when He had ascended back

into heaven, their message to the watching disciples was: "This same Jesus shall so come in like manner as ye have seen him go into heaven."

6. *It is declared by the inspired servants of God.* Which is to say, the glorification of Christ is the central theme of the Word. It is the burden of the first prophecy (Gen. 3:15), and the thrice-repeated last message from the Son of God Himself (Rev. 22). And, be it carefully noted, these chosen men who wrote the Holy Scriptures spake not their own message, but only "as they were moved by the Holy Ghost." The Lord God has not in vain filled up the pages of the Holy Book with multiplied hundreds of messages concerning the coming glorification of His Son.

7. *It is guaranteed by fulfilled prophecy.* Would God literally and perfectly fulfill all the prophecies relating to the sufferings of His Beloved Son, and then fail to do exactly as He has promised concerning His glorification? Assuredly not. Thus do the scores and hundreds of fulfilled prophecies not only proclaim God's willingness, but His ability to do as He has said.

THE MANNER OF HIS GLORIFICATION

OUTLINE FOR CHAPTER X

[God hath] given him a name which is above every name: that at the name of Jesus every knee should bow . . . and every tongue should confess that Jesus Christ is Lord (Phil. 2:9-11).

1. His glorification will be effected by His *personal* return: John 14:3; Acts 1:10, 11; Rev. 22:7, 12, 20.
2. His glorification will be effected by His *visible* return: Zech. 12:10; Matt. 24:27-30; 26:64; Luke 17:24; Acts 1:10, 11; Rev. 1:7, 8.
3. His glorification will be *marvelous, complete* and *perfect*: Heb. 2:9.
   a. *Behold the Man of Sorrows! Behold the Lord of Lords!*

"The babe wrapped in swaddling clothes."	"Clothed with a cloud, in all his glory."
"Acquainted with grief."	"Anointed with oil of gladness."
"Bowing the knee, they mocked him."	"Every knee shall bow and tongue confess: Lord of lords."
"Wearing the crown of thorns."	"Wearing the golden crown."
"So marred, beyond recognition."	"His countenance as the sun."
"He gave up the ghost."	"Alive forevermore."
"Laid in the tomb."	"On the throne of his glory."

   b. *Behold the Servant!*   *Behold the King of kings!*

"Having no comeliness, nor beauty."	"The king in his beauty, fairest of ten thousand."
"He was wearied."	"As the sun in his strength."
"Had not where to lay his head."	"Heir of kingdoms of the world, and of all things."
"Without honour."	"Worthy to receive all honour."
"[They said] he is beside himself."	"He shall be called Wonderful, Counsellor, Mighty God."

"He bare his cross [upon his shoulder]."	"The government of the world shall be on his shoulder."
"The suffering servant, obedient unto death."	"The King of kings, conqueror of death."

c. *Behold the Lamb!* / *Behold the Lion!*

"Bound and led away."	"He shall bind Satan."
"Brought into the hall of judgment."	"He shall sit in judgment upon the throne of his glory."
"Encompassed by the assembly of the wicked."	"He shall miserably destroy the wicked."
"They took up stones to cast at him."	"They cry to the stones, fall on us and hide us from his wrath."
"Clothed with a scarlet robe [in mockery]."	"Clothed with a vesture dipped in the blood of his enemies."
"Smitten with a reed."	"He shall break the nations with a rod of iron."
"They spit upon and struck his face."	"They cry, hide us from the face of him that sitteth on the throne."
"They pierced his hands."	"He comes, having in his hand a sharp sickle."
"They pierced his feet."	"His feet shall tread the winepress of God's fierce wrath."
"As a lamb . . . he opened not his mouth."	"The lion of the tribe of Judah shall roar from on high."

Note: See Appendix I, Definitions 2, 10 and 14.

In one sense the suffering Son has already become the glorified Son, seated in great honor at the right hand of the Father in heaven, after having perfectly accomplished His mission on the earth. There He receives the continuous praise and worship due Him. But what about here, on earth? Will any dare to say that the Lord Jesus Christ is being glorified on earth as He is in heaven? The answer is tragically obvious.

And so, when we speak of the coming glorification of the Lord Jesus, we speak of the *manifestation,* in great power and majesty, of *His glory* here on earth. We speak of that

time when God will force all men everywhere to render the
homage due His Blessed Son. We speak of that time when
God, the Father, will perfectly avenge all the sufferings of His
Son, when He will send Him forth as the Lion of the
tribe of Judah and no more the suffering Lamb of God.
We speak of that time when the Cross gives way to the
Crown.

1. *His glorification will be effected by His personal return.*
He personally suffered and bled and died at His first advent:
will He, then, be glorified, as it were, by proxy? Assuredly
not! What a travesty of justice would that be: to ask Him to
bear all the suffering and shame in His own person, and then
deny Him an equally *personal glorification.* "This same Jesus"
shall indeed come, *in person,* to be glorified.

2. *His glorification will be effected by His visible return.*
"Every eye shall see him." And what a spectacle that will be,
when God turns out all the lights of the heavens, creating an
utterly black background against which will flash forth the
majestic brilliance of the Sun of Righteousness arising with
healing in His wings! Tongue cannot describe, nor mind
grasp the beauty and fullness of the Great Event, that moment
when God the Son comes back personally and visibly to the
earth that rejected and killed Him.

3. *His glorification will be marvelous, complete and perfect.*
It is with a sense of futility that we endeavor to show the
absolute contrast between His sufferings and His glory. If
our present sufferings work for *us* a far greater weight of
glory, *how much more His?* What we are trying to say is
that there will be, for Him, glory multiplied for every single
minute detail of suffering. Instead of the suffering Man of
Sorrows, we behold the glorified Lord of lords. Instead of
the suffering Servant, we behold the glorified King of kings.
And instead of the suffering Lamb of God, we behold the
glorified Lion of the tribe of Judah.

THE TIME AND PLACE OF HIS GLORIFICATION

OUTLINE FOR CHAPTER XI

*In his times he shall show [the world] who is the blessed
and only Potentate, the Kings of kings, and Lord of lords
(I Tim. 6:15).*

1. The time of His glorification: Acts 17:31; I Tim. 6:14, 15.
   a. After the Rapture of the Church: Acts 15:13-17; I Thess.
      3:13; Jude 14; Rev. 19:7, 8, 14.
   b. Before the Millennium: Is. 9:6, 7; 26:9; Jer. 23:5, 6; Dan.
      7:9-14; Rev. 19:11-20:4.
   c. At earth's darkest hour: Ps. 2; Zech. 12:2, 3, 8-10; Zech.
      14:2-4; Dan. 2:44, 45; Matt. 13:36-43, 47-50; Matt. 24:21,
      29, 30; Luke 17:26-30; Luke 18:8; II Thess. 1:7-10; II
      Thess. 2:8.
2. The place of His glorification: Ps. 47:6-9; Mic. 5:4; Zech. 8:23;
   Matt. 24:30.
   a. Palestine: Deut. 32:8, 9; Is. 2:2-4; 59:20; Obad. 17.
   b. Jerusalem: Jer. 3:17; Amos 1:2; Zech. 2:10-12; Zech. 8:3;
      Mal. 3:1; Ezek. 5:5.
   c. Mount of Olives: Zech. 14:4.

Note: See Appendix I, Definitions 2, 10, 12, 14, 24, 26, and 29.
   See Appendices II and III.

To allay any fears that we are about to take off down the
unscriptural path of "date-setting," let it be noted that we are
concerned with "the time" of His glorification as related to
other events. Will it be before or after the Millennium? Before or after the home-going (rapture) of the Church? And
what conditions may be expected to prevail on earth at the
moment of His return?

1. The time of His glorification. First it is a set time, an

appointed day. No man can possibly know the exact day or hour, but the point to remember is that it is already *set*.

a. After the Rapture of the Church. The Church is His Body, of which He is the Head; she is the Bride, and He is the Bridegroom. At this point it should be noted that His glorious return will be immediately preceded by the greatest period of judgment ever to overtake the world (Matt. 24: 21-30). This raises a most vital question: Will His Bride, the Church, have to be on earth when God's great judgment-wrath strikes, or will Christ come for her before this great Tribulation? To ask is to answer; because it is perfectly obvious that He will never have to experience again God's wrath against sin, and the Church is one with Him, His Body, His Bride; meaning that if she suffers, He suffers (as He clearly indicated when He asked Saul, the persecutor of the Church, "Saul, Saul, why persecutest thou me?"). We do not wonder, therefore, that He has promised to deliver His beloved from the wrath to come (I Thess. 1:10 and Rev. 3:10). Further, the Scriptures cited confirm this by predicting that He will come with His saints, all of them, to be glorified. And to come *with* them, He must *first* come for them. Thus it is established as both reasonable and Scriptural that the Church *must* be caught up to be with Him *before* the great Tribulation and *before* His glorious personal return.

b. *Before the Millennium.* Of all the false doctrines which have robbed the Church of its testimony, power and vitality, perhaps none has been more subtle, widespread and damaging than the one which purports to teach that the Church must establish the Millennium before Christ returns in glory. So lacking is this false doctrine in Scriptural support, and so completely out of harmony with all logic and sound reasoning, that its prevalence is no less than a remarkable tribute to the deceptive power of Satan. Let us just briefly analyze the facts, in the light of both Scripture and logic.

The Millennium is the thousand years of perfect peace and

righteousness, with all the attendant blessings, promised over and over throughout the prophetic Word. Of this there can be no question. But when will this longed-for time come, and how? The post-millennialist says that it will be established by the Church before Christ returns in glory; in other words, Christ is not to return until after the Millennium. The pre-millennialist holds the opposite: that Christ will return to establish the Millennium personally, that He must come back in glory before there can be any such thing as a thousand years of perfect peace, righteousness and prosperity on this sin-cursed, war-torn earth. To state the proposition thus, would seem to settle the matter beyond any doubt. For, if there is to be a thousand years of bliss before Christ personally returns in glory it would mean that His warnings and exhortations to watch and be ready for His imminent return are meaningless, since His coming would have to be *at least* one thousand years away; it would mean that we, instead of Christ, would crush the head of the Serpent (Satan); it would mean that we, instead of Christ, would overcome and eradicate sin; it would mean that we would establish the kingdom with the King still in exile; it would mean that we would bring about world peace, with the Prince of Peace still banished and rejected; it would mean that we would cause righteousness to cover the earth as the waters cover the sea, apart from Jesus Christ the righteous; it would mean that we would bring in universal prosperity, independent of Him who is Creator and Heir of all things; in short, it would mean that we would have the glory, leaving only the sufferings to Him.

Obviously, this can never be. Not only for the reasons above cited, but for the equally clear one that sinful man is utterly incapable of bringing in the kingdom of Christ on earth. Nor did Christ ever entrust this task to the Church: she is a "stranger and pilgrim" in enemy territory, with the one mission of winning lost souls to a saving knowledge of the Lord Jesus Christ before judgment strikes a doomed world. So there is only one logical, scriptural conclusion to reach: *the Lord Jesus Christ must come personally in glory before the Millennium.*

c. *At earth's darkest hour.* "Immediately after the [unprecedented] tribulation of those days . . . they shall see the Son of man coming in the clouds of heaven with power and great glory." We say that the darkest hour is just before dawn; and so shall it be in the world preceding the "rising of the sun of righteousness with healing in his wings." In that awful seven-year period closing this present evil age, and just immediately preceding the return of Christ, this weary world will go through the most trying time of all its history; the Antichrist will hold sway in all his wickedness, and even Satan himself will personally be on the earth during the last three and one-half years, as evil reaches its hellish climax. But "when the enemy shall come in like a flood, the Spirit of the Lord shall lift up a standard against him." And that standard is none other than the blood-stained banner of the Man of Calvary as He returns in great power and glory to tread the winepress of the fierceness and wrath of Almighty God, and to take over the reins as King of kings and Lord of lords!

2. *The place of His glorification.* Of all the countless planets of God's limitless universe, this small one which we call the earth was the scene of the incarnation, sufferings and death of God the Son; it must, therefore, of necessity be the scene of His avenging glorification.

a. Of all the lands of the earth, *Palestine* (the center of this planet from God's viewpoint — Deut. 32:8, 9) was the locale of the sufferings of Christ; and thus has it been foretold in the sure Word of prophecy that "the Redeemer shall come to Zion."

b. Of all the places of Palestine, it was in *Jerusalem* that He was tried, falsely condemned and cruelly crucified. So when He returns, it will be to dwell in the midst of Jerusalem.

c. And in that day, "His feet shall stand upon the *Mount of Olives*"; that Mount upon whose slopes He agonized drops of blood in the Garden of Gethsemane; that Mount from whose summit He ascended to the Father after finishing His work on earth. How precisely, how exactly, how minutely does the Father gloriously avenge His Beloved Son!

CHAPTER XII

THE INSTRUMENT OF HIS GLORIFICATION

54

36:24-28; Hos. 2; 6:1-3; Hos. 14:4-8; Mic. 7:18-20;
Zech. 12:10; Zech. 13:1, 8, 9; Hebrews 8:8-11.
8. Israel's destiny manifested: Is. 2:2-4; 14:1, 2; 24:23; 60; 61:6;
62:1-3, 11, 12; Jer. 23:5, 6; Ezek. 36:8-15; Joel 3:18; Amos
9:11-15; Mic. 4:1, 2; Zeph. 3:14-20; Haggai 2:6-9; Zech. 8:12,
13; Zech. 8:20-23; 14:16-21; Acts 15:13-18; Rom. 11:11, 12.
Note: See Appendix I, Definitions 2, 10, 14, 16 and 26.

God has chosen to deal with man through man. Even the
Son of God became man that He might make us sons of God.
Likewise the Bible, God's revelation to man, has been given
to us through human instrumentality. And when Christ's
glory is manifested throughout all the earth, it will again be
through a human channel that God speaks to mankind. May
we firmly keep in mind the divine truth that "God's gifts and
callings are without repentance [change of mind]" (Rom. 11:
29).

1. *Israel's calling.* The passages cited in the outline are
sufficient to prove beyond cavil that Israel is indeed to be
distinguished from all other peoples of the earth in that they
are *the chosen people* insofar as God's program and plans earthward are concerned. Let it be firmly fixed in the mind that
Israel's calling is *irrevocable* and *unchangeable;* that her
calling is as of the same import as God's earthward program; that her calling is as vital as the whole plan of divine
redemption.

2. *Israel's mission.* The chosen people are the center, the
channel of God's dealings and plans earthward; and they
are thus His instrument in a threefold manner:

a. In the midst of an ever-degenerating human race, sunk
in the depths of sin and idolatry, Israel was called to bear
faithful witness to the one true God.

b. In line with this task, we are not surprised to find that
the written Word of God, the Bible, was transmitted to the
human race through Israel. All the human authors of the
Word were of Israel with the possible exception of Luke.

c. And, finally, it was through Israel that the Lord Jesus Christ came (according to the flesh); and it is also through Israel that His glorious second advent will be manifested earthward.

3. *Israel's land.* Insofar as the human element is concerned, God's dealings with man in His earthward program are through Israel, and they are through Israel *in her land.* The chosen people and the Holy Land are inseparable; and when the people are out of the land God's prophetic program is temporarily held in abeyance. And may we grasp the immutable truth that Palestine belongs to Israel forever by divine decree. Her disobedience may cause her temporary expulsion, but man can by no means in the least thwart God's purpose that Israel and Palestine must ultimately and eternally be united.

4. *Israel's disobedience and world-wide dispersion.* "Whom the Lord loveth he chasteneth." He dearly loves Israel, and hers is a high and holy calling and mission, so we are not surprised to learn from the sure Word of prophecy that God repeatedly foretold drastic punishment for disobedience. This punishment was to be effected through defeat and captivity by the Gentile nations; and continued disobedience was to bring about Israel's world-wide dispersion. The sure Word of prophecy has had its literal fulfillment, even though these are the dearly beloved and chosen people of God. First the ten northern tribes were defeated and carried captive by the cruel Assyrians; and then, more than one hundred years later, the southern kingdom of Judah was overthrown and Jerusalem and the holy Temple destroyed by Nebuchadnezzar, who carried the people captive to Babylon. True to His Word, God caused the return of a remnant to Palestine, under Ezra and Nehemiah, that Israel might be back in the land for the first advent of the Messiah. But they rejected and crucified the Son of God, and so in the year 70 A.D., as had been prophesied by both Daniel and Christ, the Romans destroyed

Jerusalem in one of the bloodiest sieges of all history; they utterly tore down the Temple so that not one stone was left on another (as Christ had foretold), and Israel was then literally dispersed among all the nations of the earth, where, down through the long centuries, her suffering and persecution has been indescribable.

5. *Israel's preservation.* God has pledged His Word: "I will not cast them away to destroy them utterly." Neither will He permit man to destroy His chosen people. To this truth all the Pharaohs, the Hamans and the Hitlers bear eloquent witness. To Abraham God promised: "I will bless them that bless thee, and curse him that curseth thee." And so has it been with individuals and nations. Just in recent years we have witnessed a most graphic illustration of this truth. Hitler cruelly put to death six million Jews; eventually he and his people felt the wrath of God. America and Britain have been foremost in befriending God's chosen people, and we verily believe that this fact is one of the basic reasons for God having delivered us in victory from the great world wars. But anti-Semitism is a powerful weapon of Satan, and we, as individuals and as a nation, need to be much exercised lest we fall prey to this wile of the Devil and bring God's wrath upon us. Let us note, with Paul, the divine verdict: "Hath God cast away his people? God forbid!" He will not, He cannot cast them away: both His pledged Word and His future program earthward demand their preservation.

6. Literally, Israel is to be *the* chosen instrument through whom the coming glorification of the returning Son of God will be manifested. The Old Testament abounds with glowing passages, telling of that glorious day when "out of *Zion* shall go forth the law, and the Word of the Lord from *Jerusalem.*"

At this point attention must be called to another widespread doctrine and belief, one as false and unreasonable as it is unscriptural. We speak of the almost universal belief in Christendom that God has indeed cast away Israel; that He is completely through with her, and that, instead, He is now working, and will ever work, only through the Church. This utterly untenable doctrine holds that all the curses of the Old Testament are Israel's, while all the blessings belong to the Church. Clear, specific and plain statements of the Word concerning Israel, Zion, Jerusalem, Palestine, etc., are spiritualized, twisted and distorted to apply to the Church and heaven, instead of to Israel and the earth. This false teaching is a logical handmaid to the doctrine of post-millennialism; for if the plain truth of Christ's literal thousand-year reign on earth, through Israel, after His glorious return, be denied, then the grave error of substituting the Church for Israel, and heaven for earth, must follow. And this inevitably leads to the social gospel and apostasy; for, if the Church must indeed bring in the kingdom without the King, and if, as is true, the majority of people continue increasingly to reject the Gospel of salvation through the shed blood of Christ, then a faster means must be sought to "bring in the kingdom." And so legislation, humanitarian schemes, and man-made devices of all sorts are undertaken in a frantic and futile effort to establish the Millennium apart from the glorious personal return of the Lord Jesus Christ. How vitally important it is to divide rightly the Word of truth. Israel has a glorious *earthly* calling and destiny; the Church has a glorious *heavenly* calling and destiny. Let us steadfastly refuse to confuse them in any wise.

7. *Israel's destiny realized.* The glorious destiny of God's chosen people will yet be realized exactly as foretold, and in the following manner:

a. *By her restoration to her land.* This is an absolute prerequisite; because, as has been pointed out, the people and the land are inseparable in God's program. To be the witness she was called to be, to the one true God, Israel had to be in Palestine; to bring forth the Messiah at His first advent, Israel had to be in Palestine; and to realize her wonderful destiny as the instrument of His glorification when He comes back, Israel must be in Palestine, the promised land.

b. *By her purging and regeneration.* But the tragedy is that it is still essentially a disobedient nation returning to her land. Generally, Israel is returning in unbelief, continuing to reject Jesus of Nazareth as her Messiah, although individual Jews are finding the salvation of their souls through faith in Him, even as do individual Gentiles during this present age of grace. Therefore, the chosen people must face their most trying of all terrible experiences ("the day of Jacob's trouble") when the purging wrath of a Holy God breaks upon them. Then, after the purging out of the rebels, the remnant will indeed become a regenerated and cleansed people, a holy nation, born-again through faith in their promised Messiah when "they shall look on him whom they have pierced."

8. *Israel's destiny manifested.* Little does a Christ-rejecting, Bible-disbelieving, skeptical world believe it, but downtrodden Israel is destined, by the sure Word of prophecy, to be "a name and a praise among all people of the earth." Because when Christ, the King of kings, returns in great power and glory to take over His rightful rulership of the world, His headquarters will be Palestine; His capital will be Jerusalem; and the head of the nations will be Israel.

God has pledged this, and so it must be. And when it does come to pass, Israel's glory, as the channel of *His* glorification, will be exceedingly dazzling in its beauty. "Then shall the moon be confounded, and the sun ashamed, when the Lord of Hosts shall reign in *Mount Zion,* and in *Jerusalem* before His ancients gloriously!" The passages cited in the outline should be carefully read in order better to appreciate the import of this profound prophecy.

Chapter XIII

THE RESULT OF HIS GLORIFICATION: JUDGMENT

While universal blessing is the ultimate object of His coming glorification, the continued prevalence and increase of sin in a Christ-rejecting world can only mean that the first effect and result of His return must be judgment. Perhaps it might help in our understanding of this neglected truth to put it this way: During this present age of grace, God is *asking* man to accept His Son as Saviour and Lord; upon their final refusal to do so, He will *force* all men everywhere to acknowledge His Lordship. Thus judgment is made inevitable by man's persistent rejection of the Christ of God. And it will fall in all its terribleness, because the Father has decreed that "all men must honour the Son."

1. *The wrath of the King of kings.* If the anger of man be awful to behold, how much more the wrath of God? Surely it is a terrible thing, for individual or nation, to fall unprepared into the hands of the living God. But that is exactly where this Christ-rejecting world is rapidly heading.

a. *Its cause.* Why would God, who is love and mercy and compassion, become angry, and vent His awful wrath on His creature? There is one, only one, answer: *sin.* God hates it with a hatred born of His perfect holiness. He gave His Son unto death for it, so that, by faith in Him, man might forever escape the wrath of a righteous God. But man says no to Christ, and so inevitable judgment must fall.

b. *Its duration.* But still, "judgment is His strange work"; He has no pleasure in the death of the wicked. So we learn from Romans 9:28 that "He will finish the work, and cut it short in righteousness: because a short work will the Lord make upon the earth." Thus it is that the final seven years of Daniel's great time-prophecy (9:24-27) is the relatively brief period during which the wrath of God, and of His Christ, will be vented on the earth. And it is particularly the last half of these seven years which is designated as the Great Tribulation.

Somewhat parenthetically we now call attention to another way in which God tempers judgment with mercy during the day of His great wrath. Revelation 7 describes the world-wide harvesting of souls for Christ through the preaching of 144,000 God-fearing, Christ-believing Jews. This, we believe, is the proclamation of the "gospel of the kingdom" in all the world for a witness unto all nations, just preceding the age-ending return of Christ in glory. This will take place during the seven year tribulation period, after the Church has been called home, and must therefore be carried on by some agency other than the Church. So God raises up a witnessing body from Israel who proclaim again the message of John the Baptist: Repent, for the kingdom is at hand (the King is about to come back). An innumerable multitude believes this message, turns to Christ, and becomes the saved nations making up the nucleus of His kingdom on earth at His return. It should be noted that these faithful witnesses from Israel will not have accepted Christ as their personal Saviour prior to the rapture of the Church, for, if they had, then they would have also been caught up, because in the Church, His Body and Bride, all distinction as to Jew and Gentile is done away. But they will turn to Christ *after* the rapture and become God's agency for the greatest and most universal evangelistic campaign ever undertaken on earth, literally preaching the Gospel to all nations as prophesied in Matthew 24:14.

c. *Its effect.* The passages cited should suffice to tell us enough about the effect of the outpouring of the wrath of God to make it clear that its horror is beyond our comprehension. Little wonder that in those days men seek death as a refuge, but in vain; and that they cry out to the rocks and mountains to fall on them and hide them from His great wrath.

2. *The return of the King of kings.* At the climax of the outpoured wrath of God, and at the peak of the all-out effort against God and God's people by Satan and Antichrist, heaven opens and in great majesty, power and glory, the King of kings and Lord of lords triumphantly returns to destroy Antichrist and all his hordes, bind Satan and set up His supreme throne in Jerusalem, from which He initiates His one

thousand-year rule by calling the nations to judgment. As the nations come before His throne they are judged on the basis of their treatment of His brethren, the faithful, believing Jews, during the Tribulation (the "day of Jacob's trouble"). Those whose attitude was merciful and kind and sympathetic toward the persecuted remnant are permitted to enter His glorious kingdom; while those who hated and mistreated them are banished into outer darkness.

3. *The rule of the King of kings.* A much misunderstood truth is that when Christ returns to set up literally and personally His kingdom on earth, He will "rule with a rod of iron." Just what is the significance of this? Surely He has to initiate His reign with such drastic measures because He finds sin at its climax and Satan at the height of his power when He returns. But it is also plain that He continues to rule with a rod of iron, and this can mean only one thing: He will force no one, even during the Millennium, to accept Him as personal Saviour (and many will refuse Him); but, on the other hand, He *will* force complete obedience to Him as King of kings. This inveterate evil of the human heart will be more fully brought out later, but Isaiah 26:9 will now be cited as a graphic comment on this profound truth: "When thy judgments are in the earth [then] will the inhabitants of the world learn righteousness." And, we might well add, not before!

Revelation 4 and 5 vividly demonstrate the truth that *only Christ* is the rightful Ruler of this world, and, until He comes, God has foretold only turmoil, strife, war and confusion ("I will overturn, overturn, overturn it" Ezek. 21:27). But when the King of kings is enthroned, then will there be a supreme, universal and everlasting kingdom on earth, such as God intended, and such as men dream about and long for. (At the end of the thousand years, there will be one last desperate effort on the part of Satan to usurp the kingdom, but this is immediately defeated by direct intervention from heaven, and the eternal supremacy of the King of kings no more challenged).

Chapter XIV

THE RESULT OF HIS GLORIFICATION: MILLENNIAL BLESSING

Another has well said: "Only by the second coming of Christ will the failure of man be undone, Satan overcome, sin uprooted, creation delivered, death abolished, redemption completed, Paradise regained, and the whole earth filled with the glory of God — only then will come the time of restitution of all things to the blessed state and condition intended by God" (Acts 3:20, 21).

1. *Nature delivered from the curse and bondage of sin.* Even Nature, having been made to share in the curse of sin,

65

groans for its deliverance; and her groanings will be heard in the day that her Maker is again enthroned. Nature's wondrous beauties now are as nothing compared to her glories in the day of her deliverance from the curse of sin.

2. *Beast delivered from the curse and bondage of sin.* "The wolf shall lie down with the lamb, and the leopard shall lie down with the kid; and the calf and the young lion and the fatling together; and a little child shall lead them." This is no figure of speech; it is the literal description of the marvelous changes that will take place in the animal world when the King of kings reigns supreme on the earth.

3. *Man delivered from the curse and bondage of sin.* The believer's soul is eternally redeemed through faith in the Lord Jesus Christ, but "we groan within ourselves, waiting for the redemption of the body," and this complete deliverance from the curse and bondage of sin will not be realized until He returns to reign.

a. *Universal righteousness.* And when Jesus Christ the righteous reigns in righteousness, then will all evil bow to justice and all sin to righteousness. Then will there be established universal righteousness, which is the only foundation sufficient for universal peace and universal prosperity.

b. *Universal peace.* "Swords into plowshares . . . spears into pruning-hooks . . . war no more." Again we say that these are not figurative phrases; they are literal portrayals of what it will be like on earth, on all the earth, when the Prince of Peace is at last enthroned.

c. *Universal prosperity.* In righteousness and peace, safety and security, *every* man shall sit under *his* fig tree, and under *his* vine. There will be an abundance of plenty, banishing all fear as to hunger or suffering of any kind. And every man shall long enjoy the work of his hands, released from the grim specter of seeing it snatched away by the grim reaper, Death. Literally, Paradise regained!

Chapter XV

THE RESULT OF HIS GLORIFICATION: VICTORY ETERNAL

1. *Final victory.* The very fact that Christ rules with "a rod of iron" during His millennial kingdom on earth is sufficient to indicate that victory, final and eternal, is not fully accomplished at His return in the sense that all potential sin and

evil is then fully eradicated and destroyed. Evil would still rear its ugly head if permitted, and thus "He must reign till He hath put all things under His feet." This is to in no wise detract from the bliss of the millennial kingdom: He will insure its perfections with the "rod of iron" stretched forth against any and all wickedness which might try to assert itself openly. But the all-seeing eye of God looks down into the heart and sees, in multitudes living in the glorious kingdom, sin yearning to express itself against the Lord and against His Christ. And this potential rebellion must be brought into the open and once-for-all dealt with before the final doom of Satan, sin and death is sounded. Then, and only then, will Christ have won the final and complete victory in the "conflict of the ages."

a. *The final rebellion*. At the return of the Lord Jesus Christ, Satan is bound for one thousand years so that he might not deceive the nations during Christ's millennial reign. At the close of the *Millennium*, he is loosed for a brief season, and immediately a great innumerable host from the four corners of the earth follows him in one last desperate assault against the authority and rulership of the Christ of God, as He rules the earth from His throne in Jerusalem. The apostasy is complete, so no message of grace, no invitation to repentance, is sent forth from God, but only terrible, direct, all-consuming judgment from an angry heaven.

How could Satan, as great deceiver as he admittedly is, delude multiplied millions into an open rebellion against the King of kings Himself? It is beyond our full comprehension, but perhaps Jeremiah 17:9 furnishes the clue: "The heart is deceitful about all things, and desperately wicked," and is capable of any evil if not surrendered to Christ the Saviour.

b. *The final judgment*. We now approach perhaps the most solemn and awesome scene in all the Word of God: the Great White Throne Judgment. Time has ended, giving place to never-ending eternity; the earth and heaven are fled away from so horrible a sight; the Judge ascends the Great White Throne; all the wicked dead are resurrected and summoned to stand before the bar; the Book of Life is opened; other books are opened; the judgment begins.

The first one is called by name; he takes his place before the great Judge; the Book of Life is searched for his name, but it cannot be found — only a terrible blank where the name might have been. The other books are searched: every thought, word, deed and action of that miserable one's whole life is faithfully on record. The Book of Life, by the absence of his name, seals his doom; the other books determine the measure of his eternal punishment; and the Great Judge pronounces the fateful verdict from which there is no appeal: to the everlasting Lake of Fire. The next one is summoned, and the next, and the next; till all who have died without the saving grace of the Lord Jesus Christ have been banished to the Lake of Fire, the second death.

c. *The final victory.* And now Christ is prepared to deliver up the kingdom to the Father that God may be all in all. He has reigned with a rod of iron and has crushed all contrary rule and authority. His enemies have all been overthrown; Satan and all his followers have been eternally consigned to the Lake of Fire; Death has been destroyed; and the earth and heavens made new, purged from all the curse and stain of sin. God is unchallenged on His throne, and perfect peace and righteousness reign supreme.

2. *Eternity.* If we are unable to grasp fully the wonders of prophecy as related to time, how much more marvelous is the vista of eternity as we view the unending "ages of the ages"! As Paul says in I Corinthians 2:9, 10, we have not seen, heard or even thought about the wonder of the things that God has prepared for them that love Him; *but God hath revealed them unto us by His Spirit.* Which is to say that the sure Word of prophecy is so powerful a telescope as to pierce the veil that separates time from eternity, and give us a

glimpse of what it will be like to be forever with "the One who inhabiteth eternity." Although we can now, in the flesh, see only as through a glass darkly, still the view is breath-taking in its grandness and beauty.

There is still heaven and earth, but new! Maybe a new creation; or maybe the old completely renewed; but, in either event, the result is the same. Dominating the scene is the Holy City, New Jerusalem, coming down from God out of heaven, prepared as a bride adorned for her husband. Whether the language be literal or figurative, or some of both, the spectacle is breath-taking! New Jerusalem: a glittering diamond cube, measuring some fifteen hundred miles in all directions, surrounded with a mighty wall of pure diamond which rests on foundations of precious stones; having great doors of individual pearls; streets of gold so pure as to be transparent; and lightened with the glory light of God and the Lamb, from whose throne eternally flows the pure river of the water of life.

And we, His blood-bought children, are *there*, with Him! We shall see His face! His name shall be in our foreheads! We shall serve Him! And we shall reign with Him forever and ever!

PART IV

This Present Evil Age:
Prophecy Being Fulfilled

Chapter XVI

THE SEQUENCE OF THE AGES

The worlds were framed [ages were planned — Scofield]
by the word of God (Heb. 11:3).

1. The ages past: Eph. 3:5.
    a. The age of innocence: Ending in expulsion from the Garden of Eden. (Gen. 2:15-17; 3:23, 24)
    b. The age of conscience: Ending in the universal flood. (Gen. 6:5-7; 7:17-24)
    c. The age of brotherhood — one people, one language, one speech: Ending in the confusion of tongues at Babel. (Gen. 11:1-9)
    d. The age of promise: Ending in bondage in Egypt. (Gen. 12:1-3; Ex. 1:13, 14)
    e. The age of law: Ending in Calvary (and Israel's world-wide dispersion). (Ex. 19:1-8; 20:1-20; Matt. 27:35; Luke 21:20-24)
2. The ages to come: Eph. 2:7.
    a. The age of the kingdom (Christ's thousand-year reign on earth): Ending in the final rebellion and final judgment. (Rev. 20)
    b. The "ages of the ages" (eternity): Never-ending. (Heb. 1-8; Rev. 22:5)
3. The age of grace ("this present evil age"): John 1:17; Gal. 1:4.
    a. Its character (parenthetical — between the Cross and the Crown): Dan. 9:26; Acts 15:13-17.

   b. Its ruler: Matt. 11:12; II Cor. 4:3, 4; Eph. 2:2; 6:12; I John
      5:19.
   c. Its nature: John 1:11 and Mark 15:12, 13; Acts 3:12-15; Gal.
      1:4; Eph. 5:16; James 3:16.
   d. Its witness: Matt. 16:18; Acts 1:8.
   e. Its course and end: Matt. 13:36-43; 47-50; Matt. 24:3, 21;
      II Thess. 2:1-12; II Tim. 3:13.
Note: See Appendix I, Definitions 3 and 22.

"Through faith we understand that the worlds were
framed [the ages were planned - *Scofield*] by the word of
God" (Heb. 11:3). Isaiah confirms this by speaking of "the
purpose that is purposed upon the whole earth" (Is. 14:26).
God is a God of order, purpose and precision; He has a
definite program earthward, perfect and complete; He knows
the end from the beginning; His hand still grips the controls
of the universe. Disorder and confusion, now so prevalent
on this planet, are the natural fruits of sin, permitted by an
all-wise Sovereign, who still overrules in all things, saying,
"thus far but no farther."

We are living in an "age" - a definite period of time, with a
pre-written beginning, course and end according to the sure
Word of prophecy. There have been "ages past"; there will
be "ages future." And so better to understand what we mean
by "this present evil age," we shall do well to consider briefly
these "ages," or "dispensations." (Dr. C. I. Scofield defines
an age or dispensation as "a period of time during which man
is tested in respect of obedience to some specific revelation of
the will of God.")

1. *The ages past.* Inasmuch as our purpose now is to study
rather closely this present age, we will refrain from lengthy
discussion of the five ages past, although it should be noted
carefully that, under all the varying conditions, and in all
these testings, man invariably failed miserably to heed the
Lord and each age ended in failure and judgment. A study
of the Scriptures cited in the outline, along with other per-
tinent passages, will prove highly profitable and we strongly

suggest that this be done by anyone interested in knowing more about the ways of God with man.

2. *The ages to come.* Having briefly looked back, we now glance forward to the future ages, the ones to follow our present one. Actually there is only one more age in the strict sense of the word, and that is the glorious millennial kingdom age when Christ reigns on earth following His glorious return. As has already been noted at some length, even this blessed period ends in failure and horrible judgment. Then comes eternity, which has been designated in the Word, "the ages of the ages." Time is no more, but in some sense it seems that there will be an unending succession of blissful ages forever and ever, utterly apart from any tinge of sin or failure of any kind.

3. *The age of grace ("this present evil age").* We live in an age which is no less definite in its beginning, course and ending than the five ages past, or the kingdom age yet to come.

a. *Its character.* We might well describe our present age as a great parenthesis, embracing all that period of time between the Cross and the Crown, between the sufferings and the glory. It is to be recalled that in Daniel 9:24-27 we find God's whole timetable for the consummation of His entire program earthward; but when 483 of the allotted 490 years had expired, Christ was rejected and crucified. This crime of the ages served to stop the prophetic clock, and, in the meantime, God permits the age of grace to run its course while He freely offers salvation to any and all who will accept the Lord Jesus Christ as personal Saviour.

b. *Its ruler.* The Prince of Peace offered Himself, but, when He came unto His own, His own received Him not. He was rejected, crucified, and, as it were, banished from this planet by sinful man. Then who is the ruler of this age? The Word saith: "The whole world lieth in the wicked one." He,

Satan, is the "ruler of this age." The kingdom of heaven suffereth violence, and the violent taketh it by force.

And so it was. Christ came, the King appeared, the kingdom was at hand; but, through wicked man, Satan violently snatched it away from its rightful Ruler, and now holds sway. God could have, of course, stopped the Devil in his course of opposition, but the salvation of lost men necessitated Calvary, and so Satan is allowed to rule temporarily at the insistent demand of sinful mankind. But powerful as Satan is, God is still the omnipotent One: Satan may rule, but the Almighty overrules.

c. *Its nature.* On the one hand it is truly the age of grace, because wicked men are offered full and free salvation by simply putting their trust in the Lamb of God slain from the foundation of the world. But it is essentially this present *evil* age. Born at Calvary, ruled by Satan, and increasingly denying the Lord that bought them, what else could it be than a wicked dispensation?

d. *Its witness.* Never since sin entered the race has God been without a witness on this earth. There must be someone to bear witness for God so that any who will might be saved. Down through the ages past, Adam, Seth, Enoch, Noah, Abraham, Israel and many others bore witness to the one true God. And in this age, which grew out of the Cross, God has His witness, the Church, the Body and Bride of Christ.

e. *Its course and end.* Contrary to the widespread belief that the task of the Church is to convert the whole world and bring in the kingdom (apart from the personal return of the King), the Word of prophecy specifically and unequivocally declares that this *evil* age will grow worse and worse, and will end in the greatest judgment of all. The Scriptures cited in the outline are more than sufficient to prove this conclusion beyond cavil.

Chapter XVII

THE WITNESS OF THIS AGE

what against thee, because thou hast left thy first love."

b. Smyrna, signifying the period of persecution and martyrdom: Rev. 2:8-11.
   (1) Duration: About 170 to 300 A.D.
   (2) Characteristics: poverty; tribulation; persecution; faithful unto death.
   (3) Christ's attitude: "These things saith the first and the last, which was dead, and is alive."
   (4) Christ's message: "Fear none of those things which thou shalt suffer . . . I will give thee a crown of life."

c. Pergamos, signifying the period of worldly corruption: Rev. 2:12-17.
   (1) Duration: about 300 to 600 A.D.
   (2) Characteristics: "Thou dwellest even where Satan's seat is [settled down in the world; married to the world]"
   (3) Christ's attitude: "He which hath the sharp sword with two edges."
   (4) Christ's message: "Repent; or else I will come unto thee quickly . . . with the sword of my mouth."

d. Thyatira, signifying the period of the papacy and Roman Catholic idolatry: Rev. 2:18-29.
   (1) Duration: about 600 to 1500 A.D.
   (2) Characteristics: "Thou sufferest that woman Jezebel, which calleth herself a prophetess, to teach and to seduce my servants to commit fornication."
   (3) Christ's attitude: "The Son of God, who hath his eyes like unto a flame of fire."
   (4) Christ's message: "I will cast . . . them . . . into great tribulation, except they repent of their deeds."

e. Sardis, signifying the period of the Protestant Reformation: Rev. 3:1-6.
   (1) Duration: about 1500 to 1750 A.D.
   (2) Characteristics: "A name that thou livest, and art dead."
   (3) Christ's attitude: "He that hath the seven Spirits of God."
   (4) Christ's message: "I will come on thee as a thief."

f. Philadelphia, signifying the period of the evangelistic zeal of the true Church within professing Christendom: Rev. 3:7-13.
   (1) Duration: about 1750 A.D. to the Rapture.
   (2) Characteristics: "Thou hast . . . kept my word, and hast not denied my name."

       (3) Christ's attitude: "He that openeth, and no man shutteth."

       (4) Christ's message: "I will keep thee from the hour of temptation."

   g. Laodicea, signifying the period of apostasy in Christendom: Rev. 3:14-19.

       (1) Duration: about 1900 A.D. to her end during the Great Tribulation.

       (2) Characteristics: lukewarm, proud, *self*-satisfied.

       (3) Christ's attitude: "The faithful and true witness."

       (4) Christ's message: "I will spue thee out of my mouth."

Note: See Appendix I, Definitions 6, 7, 9, 12, 17, 22, 29 and 30. See Appendix III.

"I will build my church" (Matt. 16:18); thus did our Lord foretell the coming of the witness who would speak to men for God during "this present evil age." And, He added, "the gates of hell shall not prevail against it"; it shall accomplish that for which it has been brought into existence.

1. *The nature of the Church.* In Matthew 13:45, 46, Christ spoke of the one pearl of great price, for which He gave everything. This is a beautiful picture of the nature of the Church. Just as the pearl comes from the wound in the oyster, so did His pearl of great price come from His pierced side, "born of water and of blood," and thus is the Church literally a part of Him — His Body. And having been, as it were, taken from His side, she is also His Bride — foreshadowed by the creation of Eve from the side of Adam. Likewise, the Church, His Body and Bride, is "the temple (habitation) of God" — not a literal building or edifice, not a man-made organization, but *one living organism.* The true Church of Jesus Christ is, therefore, that one, invisible Body, made up of every one who has been born again through personal faith in His atoning death and resurrection, whether that one be Jew or Gentile, bond or free, rich or poor, ignorant or learned, black or white, young or old. The Body is *one* — and He is the Head!

2. *The position of the Church*. The Church lives in a world which rejected and crucified her Lord! The basic importance of this fact cannot be overestimated. The Body of Jesus Christ must be a stranger and foreigner in the world that would not even offer Him a place to lay His head. And the world hates the true Church, as it hated her Lord. The Church is literally as "sheep among wolves." The tragic fact that the professing church (Christendom) has committed adultery against Christ by an unholy marriage with the world, by settling down in the world and minding earthly things, by no means diminishes the force of the truth concerning separation.

3. *The mission of the Church*. During "this present evil age," the Church has one task: to bear faithful witness everywhere to the saving grace of the crucified, risen and ascended Son of God, pleading with men, in Christ's stead, to be reconciled to God through Christ while it is still the day of salvation. Her one mission, her one message is faithfully and persistently to cry out to all men everywhere: "Behold the Lamb of God which taketh away the sin of the world."

And as she proclaims this message, she is to warn men to flee now to Christ from the wrath to come, even as Enoch of old. She is continually to warn men of the coming judgment so that they will turn to Christ while the door of grace is still open.

And as she witnesses and warns, she is to do so in the power, purity and comfort of her Blessed Hope: ever watching and waiting for her Lord to come and receive her unto Himself. Thus as she witnesses, she warns; and as she witnesses and warns, she watches heaven for the coming of the Bright and Morning Star. This, according to the Word, is the true mission of the true Church of Christ.

4. *The destiny of the Church*. To be delivered from the judgment-wrath to come, to be caught up to meet her Lord in the air and forever be with Him, to be like Him, to share

in all that is His, to reign forever with Him after returning with Him in glory to earth. In short, to conquer
death through Him who is the life and to enjoy, with Him,
all the indescribable blessings of *life eternal*. This heavenly
destiny of the Church will be realized through His coming *for*
her (I Thess. 4:13-18), and this is distinctly her blessed hope.

5. *The pre-written history of the Church-age.* Is there no
message in the sure Word of prophecy concerning the manner in which the church fulfills or fails to fulfill, her
appointed mission? To be sure there is. The second and
third chapters of Revelation contain the *pre-written history
of the professing church,* graphically and completely. After
envisioning the glorified Christ, and receiving his commission
to write "the things which thou hast seen, and the things
which are, and the things which shall be hereafter," the
Apostle John proceeds, in chapters 2 and 3, to give the inspired
prophecy of the whole course of the church age. . ."the things
which are."

First, it should be noted, these messages were to literal local
churches then existing in Asia Minor, and were specifically
for each according to the particular need of each. Also, these
messages have a real meaning and value for individual
Christians and churches today — this truth cannot be over-
emphasized. But, primarily, these seven messages constitute
a prophecy of the whole course of the professing church down
through the centuries.

It should be further noted with care, that this sevenfold
message refers to Christendom (the *professing* church, in its
outward manifestation), and not alone to the true Church.
The true Church of Jesus Christ (made up of only born-
again believers on Him) is *within* Christendom, that is, within
the sphere of the professing church. The true Church is
invisible. The professing church is visible. The professing
(visible) church, and its responsibility toward Christ, is the
burden of this great prophecy. For that reason it will be seen

that He appears to Christendom in such a manner, and with such an attitude, as befits that particular phase of her history.

This brings us to the important observation that, from "loss of first love" at the beginning to complete "apostasy" at the end, the course of the professing church is downward. Emphasizing this is the fact that, of the seven messages, five are of a critical and warning nature, while only two (to Smyrna and Philadelphia) are otherwise. This is understandable and highly significant when we realize that Smyrna typified that awful period when Satan tried unsuccessfully to blot out the Church of Christ through bloody persecution, and before he, with infinitely more success, changed his tactics and seduced the professing church into unholy wedlock with the wicked world that killed her Lord (Pergamos). Philadelphia is typical of the true church on earth in the last days of the church age, the present days of terrible evil and peril. To these two, Smyrna the persecuted and Philadelphia in the midst of universal apostasy, Christ speaks only words of comfort, cheer and hope. How meaningful is this for *us*. because doubtless the true Church is in the "Philadelphia" phrase, and His coming for us must be exceedingly nigh!

Attention should also be called to the fact that no one phase of the church's history abruptly and completely ends, with all of its particular characteristics utterly done away with, as a new phase begins. Rather is it true that each phase is predominantly characterized by the conditions indicated. For example, Smyrna, while *the* persecuted church, is not alone in her sufferings for Christ; there have been those persecuted for His Name down through all the church's history, and even until today. But that was *the* period dominated by persecution. Then, it might be pointed out that while the Philadelphian phase of world-wide evangelistic zeal began to give way to the Laodicean apostasy about 1900 A.D., Philadelphia (the true church) still continues to exist within professing Christendom and will do so until raptured by the Lord. So also do the worldly corruption of

Pergamos and the Roman Catholic idolatry of Thyatira and the dead formalism of Sardis continue until today, even to the finding of their fruition in the apostasy of Laodicea.

Thus it is clear that the professing church approaches the end of its earthly course with Philadelphia and Laodicea co-existing, but with the latter predominant as the apostasy continues apace, while the true Church (Philadelphia) remains loyal to Christ and His Word, although it becomes increasingly the minority element in Christendom.

Chapter XVIII

THE END OF THIS AGE PREVIEWED

The nearer we come to the end of this age, the more will its predicted consummation be disbelieved by mankind generally. This tragic evidence of the deluding power of Satan, "the god of this age," is manifested by the highly significant prophecy of II Peter 3:3, 4: "There shall come in the last days scoffers, walking after their own lusts, and saying, Where is the promise of his coming? for since the fathers fell asleep, all things continue as they were from the beginning of the creation." The Apostle Peter, under the inspiration of the Holy Spirit, then goes on in this vital chapter so full of prophetic truth to show that men are "willingly ignorant" of

82

the fact that there was a catastrophic age-ending Flood in the days of Noah, and that it was as little expected as is judgment today. Further, he explains that the foretold judgment, the Day of the Lord, is being held back only by the longsuffering and mercy of a God of love, who is not willing that any should perish, but that all should come to repentance. "But the day of the Lord will come as a thief in the night," in all its terrifying outpouring of the divine wrath. All past ages have ended; so will this present one. All past ages have ended in man's failure and God's judgment; so will this present one.

1. *The end foretold*. Having received ample notice from Israel that they would officially and unequivocably reject Him as the promised Messiah, and knowing this and all things aforetime, the omniscient Christ, in Matthew 13, delivers a series of parables which describe the "kingdom of heaven" during the absence of the king. His literal earthly kingdom having been postponed until His return in glory, the "kingdom of heaven" during "this present evil age" is actually what we call Christendom (or the whole sphere of professing Christianity).

For our present purpose we call attention only to the second parable, which our Lord explains in verses 36-43 by demonstrating that the age will end, and will end in judgment, because the world will increasingly reject the true Christ, even to the point of accepting the Antichrist in the last days. This judgment-ending of the age is that mentioned in Daniel 9:27 and corresponds with the last seven years of that great time-prophecy. It is likewise referred to in Matthew 24:3, Matthew 28:20 and other passages, where an erroneous translation renders it "end of the world."

2. *The end described*. (Daniel 9:24-27) clearly intimates that the end will be in judgment; Christ (Matt. 24:9-26) adds a number of details to the description of the judgment-ending, which He says will be a time of unprecedented tribulation; and John, beginning with Revelation 6 through 19:6 fills up

the picture of the wrath of God being poured out on a Christ-rejecting world. We are not sure whether Revelation 6 is a "nut-shell" preview of the whole seven-year tribulation, or a description of just the first in the series of judgments. But even though we cannot now fully understand all the details of these end-time judgments, we are permitted to understand definitely what will take place just as the curtain is raised on a doomed world following the homegoing of the true Church — this is the message of Revelation 6. And though these judgments cannot affect the raptured Church in heaven, we feel that it is vital to know something of the way the age will end, because "coming events do cast their shadows before."

By way of introduction, it should be noted that Revelation 4 and 5 describe scenes in heaven following the Rapture of the Church, and just preceding the Tribulation on earth. The glorified Christ is seen to be the only One worthy and able to take over the title-deed to the earth: He made it and bought it back at the cost of His shed blood. Having received the deed from His Father He proceeds to assert His rightful ownership by opening the seals; and as each one is opened the earth is made to feel the impact of the righteous wrath of God and His Christ.

The effect of the opening of the first seal seems to be harmless enough. A rider comes forth on a white horse, and evidently conquers through peaceable means as the bow in his hand does not appear to be fitted with an arrow. And who might this one be? None other than the Antichrist, obtaining the homage of the world through deceit and subtlety, and offering world peace to a war-weary race. He will be the Great Dictator that a desperate world is now seeking, to lead it out of the present "distress and perplexity." Christ came in the Father's Name, and the world rejected Him; He predicted that if another should come in his own name, him they would receive, and so it shall be.

But when they joyously say "peace and safety," then comes

"sudden destruction" (I Thess. 5:1-3). The faked peace is short-lived, for the opening of the next seal signals the outbreak of the greatest and most widespread war this world has ever experienced. And, as the third and fourth seals are opened, unprecedented famine, pestilence, disease and death inevitably follow.

The breaking of the fifth seal likewise reveals a dark scene, as the persecuted servants of God cry out for relief and avenging. Who are these? Certainly not the Church, now safely with Him in heaven. They are some of the faithful Jewish evangels who will proclaim the Gospel of the kingdom (Matt. 24:14) throughout the whole world during those awful days, calling on men to repent because the King is about to return. A great multitude believes their message and turns to God, but other multitudes, sin-hardened and Satan-deluded, reject these messengers and persecute them unto the death.

As the sixth seal is opened, nature responds to the call of her Creator to pour out her pent up wrath on a sin-laden world. A-bombs and H-bombs and all the other devilish inventions of sinful man are but faint shadows of what it will be when the God of the atom unleashes the forces of nature in His righteous anger. No wonder "the earth shall reel to and fro like a drunkard" (Is. 24:19, 20), and "men shall call on the rocks and mountains to fall on them."

And against this utterly black background, at the height of man's sinfulness and God's great wrath, the Lord Jesus Christ, the "Sun of Righteousness," suddenly flashes forth from heaven in all His glory, "as the lightning shineth out of the east even unto the west," to ring down the curtain on man's day (of evil) and usher in the Day of the Lord. This, in brief, is a picture of the end of the age.

3. *The end heralded.* Having learned from the sure Word of prophecy that this age will end, and how it will end, we now ask: Can we know when this age-ending is about to

take place? Or rather, perhaps we should first ask, Do we have a right to seek an answer to this question?

Our Lord severely rebuked the Scribes and Pharisees for not having discerned the signs of the times which heralded His first advent (Matt. 16:1-3), and are we to invite this same rebuke by closing our eyes to the multiplied signs of His imminent return? A wicked world has been told that the Day of the Lord will overtake it as a thief in the night, entirely unexpected; "But we, brethren, are not in darkness, that that day should overtake us as a thief" (I Thess 5·4). Are we to grope in the darkness of the wicked when we have available the blessed light of the sure Word of prophecy? Finally, our Lord (Matt. 24:33) admonishes: "When ye shall see all these things, know that he is near, even at the doors." While most wholeheartedly bowing to Matthew 24:36, which warns against date-setting, we ask, nevertheless, by what right do we fail to obey the specific command of our Lord to *know* by certain foretold signs that His coming is near? Date-setting is evil, destructive and certainly not of the Holy Spirit, because entirely unscriptural. But to know that His return is *near*, while by no means attempting to set the exact time, is one of the Word's most powerful incentives to consecrated, happy, sacrificial living on the part of the enlightened believer. Thus we conclude that we have not only the right, but an injunction from our Lord, to *know* that the end of the age, and His return, is heralded by certain signs which have been faithfully recorded in the Word of prophecy.

And now to return to our first question: How can we know that His coming draweth nigh? Jeremiah 6:4 says, "The shadows of the evening are stretched out," meaning that "coming events cast their shadows before." Amos 5:18-20 and Zephaniah 1:15, 16 confirm what we have already learned, that the end of the age will be a black day in the world's history, a day of unspeakable darkness and gloominess, full of evil men, and the fury of a Holy God. And here lies the basic answer to our question: Such an unparalleled catastrophe as the judgment-ending of this age *must* in various ways betray its approach with many telltale signs.

In order understandably to study these prophetic signs in the light of things transpiring before our very eyes, let us liken the consummation of the age unto a great drama about to be enacted. And to discern how close it may be to curtain time, we shall consider:

1. The Setting of the Stage.
2. The Assembling of the Cast.
3. The Sounding of the Prelude.

Chapter XIX

THE SETTING OF THE STAGE

Note: See Appendix I, Definition 22.

1. *One world*. While it is true the world is badly split ideologically between East and West, nevertheless modern inventions have served so to draw together the four corners of the earth that man's thinking, planning and talking is now in terms of "the whole world," and this is in striking conformity to the language of Revelation as that great book of prophecy describes the end-time drama.

2. *A sin-laden world*. It is sin that brings down the judgment wrath of God. And as the Day approaches, the world's cup of wickedness will be full to overflowing.

3. *A materialistic world*. That's the way it was in the days of Noah, just preceding the awful flood, and our Lord said it would be the same way in the end of this age. Things spiritual are cast aside: man is interested only in the material things of this life. Is not this the case today — so much so that even some thoughtful people who are not Christians are decrying the conditions?

4. *A proud world*. Pride caused the fall of Lucifer, so that he became Satan and brought sin into the world. He is the "god of this age," the father of all out of Christ, and his children increasingly manifest this family trait.

5. *A worldly-wise world*. This is a rather ambiguous phrase, but we believe it expresses the thought implied in the passages cited. As the end draws nigh, man becomes increasingly wise, but only in the wisdom of the world. And this is in God's sight as foolishness because "the fear of the Lord is the beginning of wisdom," and that fear is notably absent among the wise of this world.

6. *A selfish world*. Every man seeketh his own. Or, in our modern slang, every man "looks out for number one." This is another prominent part of the scenery on the world stage at the end-time, and one can hardly deny that selfishness is a predominant trait in people generally today.

7. *A self-satisfied world*. This is a normal outgrowth of some of the traits already mentioned. There is little feeling of

humility and dependence upon God on the part of mankind today. In time of great distress they may cry out, but otherwise He is neither considered nor consulted: man is sufficient unto himself.

8. *A pleasure-loving world.* We might very truthfully call this the age of pleasures; not that men are happy, but that they are almost constantly pursuing happiness in vain through these fleeting "pleasures for a season."

9. *An ungodly world.* The passages cited indicate organized atheism as one of the terrible evils of the end-time drama. This is the natural outcome of ignoring and rejecting God and His Christ — there must inevitably result open and active opposition to and hatred of God.

10. *A deceitful world.* Lying, cheating, misrepresentation, false witness, double-talk, fraud, truce-breaking etc. — this we see and hear on every hand till we sometimes wonder if truth shall be entirely banished from the earth. But what more to expect? Satan, the liar and father of the lie, is the "ruler of this age."

11. *A deluded world.* If the truth be forsaken, delusion, with all its attendant sorrows, must reign. Most tragic of all, however, is the way in which Satan, the deceiver, is so marvelously succeeding in deluding men by the millions into refusing the free gift of salvation through Christ and thus losing their eternal souls. And because men willfully believe the liar instead of the Truth, God has foretold that He will send upon them strong delusion in the day of judgment so that they will believe the most unbelievable lies. This is to be their terrible, but just, recompense.

12. *A cynical world.* Cynicism is the handmaid to delusion. The deluded individual shrugs his shoulder, throws up his hands and says, in effect, "So what?" For some peculiar reason this awful trait seems to be somewhat of a mark of distinction in the circles of the worldly-wise; but essentially it is another sign pointing to the end.

13. *A hypocritical world.* The world abounds today in a "veneer of religion." The profession is high-sounding, but there is no possession. The sepulcher is beautifully white on the outside, but full of dead men's bones within. These people honor God with their lips, but their heart is far from Him.

14. *A cruel world.* As the stage-setting progresses, the scenes take on an ever darker hue. Sow the wind and reap the whirlwind. From violence within the sanctity of the home, to the unspeakable cruelty of modern warfare between federations of nations, this end-time trait is increasingly in evidence.

15. *A lawless world.* Disobedient to parents, disobedient to duly appointed governmental authority, disobedient to all the Law of God, sin-hardened man wants no restraint from man or God, and more and more seeks to throw off these shackles as the end approaches.

16. *A dangerous world.* Paul begins that great end-time prophecy in II Timothy 3 by saying, "This *know* also, in the last days perilous times shall come." And these perils are greatly accentuated by modern inventions both of peace and war. Quite likely Joel and Nahum, in the passages cited, had reference centuries ago to this "mechanical age."

17. *A frightened world.* Despite the outward appearance of calm, cynicism and self-satisfaction, man today is a terribly frightened creature. Literally, "Men's hearts are failing them for fear." The A-bomb alone, with all the horror it portends, is sufficient to make this the "age of fear," but this is just one of many factors contributing to the well justified fright experienced by the Godless multitudes.

18. *A restless world.* The prophet truly said, "The wicked are like the troubled sea, when it cannot rest, whose waters cast up mire and dirt. There is no peace. . .to the wicked" (Is. 57:20, 21). As never before in the world's history do we see this restlessness of the wicked, as modern means of trans-

portation afford increasing opportunities for constant "running to and fro" over the whole face of the globe.

19. *A perplexed world.* In every phase of life in this complicated modern world, there is perplexity and distress; but especially is this true of the nations in their dealings with each other. Every effort to solve the present dilemma only seems to increase the perplexity and distress. But what else could be expected? He, the Prince of Peace, who is the only wise God, the mighty Counsellor, is forbidden a seat at the counsel table around which the nations continue vainly to gather.

20. *A desperate world.* One scene remains to complete the stage, and it seems ready to fall in place momentarily. That is the desperation that will cause a sinful, deluded, frightened and perplexed world to open its arms to the Antichrist. He is the first actor to appear when the curtain rises after the Rapture, and it is hard to believe that even so sinsick a world as this could accept such a one as its ruler unless it were reduced to the most desperate straits imaginable. And that is the very condition we see rapidly crystalizing before our very eyes today. Surely, the end must be near; our call to meet Him in the air must be nearer still!

Chapter XX

THE ASSEMBLING OF THE CAST: ANTICHRIST

OUTLINE FOR CHAPTER XX

I am come in my Father's name, and ye receive me not: if another shall come in his own name, him ye will receive (John 5:43).

1. His nationality: Dan. 7:7, 8; 9:26; Rev. 13:1-5; Rev. 17:8-11.
2. His nature: Dan. 7:8; 9:26, 27; 11:36-39; II Thess. 2:3, 4; Rev. 6:2.
3. His power: II Thess. 2:9, 10; Rev. 13; Rev. 17:12, 13.
4. His duration: Dan. 9:27; Rev. 13:5.
5. His doom: Dan. 11:45; II Thess. 2:7, 8; Rev. 17:13, 14; Rev. 19:19, 20; Rev. 20:10.

Note: See Appendix I, Definitions 4, 22 and 28.

There are as many antichrists as there are those who deny and oppose the one true Christ. But these are all, even the most wicked of them, only faint foreshadows of *the* Antichrist. As our last study so clearly indicated, the stage is apparently almost set, the Rapture of the Church is imminent. Then comes the breaking of the first seal of Revelation 6 as the end-time drama (the consummation of the age) begins. Upon the opening of this first seal, a rider comes forth on a white horse, "conquering and to conquer." It is this sinister being that we now briefly consider in the penetrating light of the sure Word of prophecy.

1. *His nationality.* Can this coming world dictator be identified as to his nationality? We verily believe so, for in Daniel 9:24-27, that great time-prophecy, it is foretold that *after* the crucifixion of the Messiah, Jerusalem will be over-

thrown by "the people of the prince to come." This destruction
of the holy city was literally carried out by the Romans in
70 A.D., as Daniel had predicted and as Christ had confirmed
in Matthew 24 and Luke 21.

An analysis of Daniel 11:37 would seem to indicate that
Antichrist will also be a Jew ("not regarding the God of his
fathers"). Devout and worthy Bible scholars are not in full
accord on this interpretation and so we refuse to be dogmatic;
but we are strongly inclined to the belief that this evil person
will be a Jew arising out of the revived Roman Empire, because he is, essentially, the *counterfeit Christ,* and Satan's
counterfeits are always exceedingly accurate imitations.

2. *His nature.* His very name betrays his true nature: Antichrist. He is in all respects, and at every point, the false
Christ, the counterfeit Messiah. He is pre-eminently the tool
of Satan, the personification of the Devil himself. He is
the essence of wickedness, lawlessness, evil, iniquity and sin.
He is, in short, everything Satan can make of a willing
instrument.

3. *His power.* Of a satanic nature, his is also satanic power.
He employs and exercises all the power of Satan, his master,
which is supernaturally great (although inferior and always
subordinate to that of the omnipotent God). All must serve,
honor and worship him or risk forfeiture of life. Today the
world longs for a strong man, one to bring order out of the
present distress and chaos. It will, in due time, get him — *the*
dictator of all time. But what a terrible delusion awaits
deceived mankind: the one to whom they look for leadership
and deliverance will prove to be none other than *the* Antichrist, the personification of Satan! The power and ruthless-
ness of all past dictators combined will appear as child's play in
the light of the cruel reign of this satanic monster.

4. *His duration.* But, praise the Lord! this sinister being
is not divine or eternal. He is only a creature. As a matter of
fact, his terrible sway is, by the mercy of God, a relatively brief

one — seven years. All of this is made clear by the prophetic Word. From II Thessalonians 2:7, 8, we learn that Antichrist does not make his appearance until *after* the Rapture of the Church; and he is overthrown by the returning Christ when He comes back in great power and glory. The Church is raptured *before* the seven-year Tribulation, and Christ returns at its end, so the duration of the wicked one is fixed. This is likewise confirmed by Daniel 9 and Revelation 13.

5. *His doom.* It is as terrible as it is certain. Usually God raises up one human instrument to punish another; but not so in this case. This wicked one is overthrown and conquered by the Lord Jesus Christ Himself at His personal return. And he does not go to his eternal doom through the door of death, but is consigned *alive* into the Lake of Fire forever to suffer his just reward.

In concluding this meditation, we feel that attention should be called briefly to "the false prophet" of Revelation 12:11-18. We believe the first ten verses of Revelation 13 have to do with the wicked one we have been considering, the Antichrist. The question then arises, who is this other one of Revelation 13 — this one so much like the Antichrist, and so closely allied with him? And it is to be noted that he suffers the same fate: being cast alive with the Antichrist into the Lake of Fire (Rev. 19:20). So, while two personages, the two nevertheless are in a very real sense, one, and we believe this is the key to the right interpretation.

These two sinister beings, one holding sway in the political realm, and the other ruling in the religious world, along with Satan, their master, make up the trinity of Evil, as opposed to the Triune Godhead. This is perfectly logical in the light of the fact that we are dealing now with the crowning counter-feit of the arch deceiver, and he does not stop short of attempt-ing to imitate the Holy, Triune Godhead. It might be suggested that the reason the Antichrist of the political realm is given the place of prominence (rather than the one in the religious realm) is that the conception of mankind in general is that of a temporal ruler insofar as the coming of the Christ is concerned. That is what Israel sought; and that is all that man generally is interested in — not spiritual but temporal things. And Satan gives them what they want, a supreme political dictator. But the portrait of Antichrist is incomplete without the likeness of his counterpart in the religious world, the "beast" of Revelation 12:11-18, who is properly called *the* False Prophet.

Chapter XXI

THE ASSEMBLING OF THE CAST:
THE REVIVED ROMAN EMPIRE

In the great prophetic message of Luke 21, our Lord,
in verse 24, uttered a most significant statement — and one
which is of vital import for us today: "Jerusalem shall be
trodden down of the Gentiles, until the times of the Gentiles
be fulfilled." Several facts stand out. Jerusalem (meaning
Israel, the chosen nation), because of her rejection and
crucifixion of Christ, is to be punished by subjugation to the
Gentiles (the other nations, as distinguished from Israel).

This is actually a continuing punishment for continued disobedience, having begun centuries before Christ, and now prolonged and intensified because of Israel's great crime and sin at Calvary. And, finally, be it carefully noted that Gentile dominion over the chosen nation is not permanent, but will continue only "until the times of the Gentiles be fulfilled."

1. *The beginning of "the times of the Gentiles."* About 600 B.C. one of the great turning points in human history occurred, when God gave the southern kingdom of Judah into the hands of Nebuchadnezzar, king of Babylon. The ten northern tribes of Israel had long been removed into captivity by the Assyrians; finally, Judah's cup of disobedience was filled to overflowing and the God of the nations temporarily, and surely with great reluctance, transferred the authority and responsibility of leadership to the Gentiles.

2. *The appearance of "the times of the Gentiles."* Nebuchadnezzar, the mighty Babylonian monarch, and admittedly a world dictator, was evidently impressed with the profound significance of what had happened, and, following his meditations thereon, he fell asleep one night and had a most fascinating dream. It was finally Daniel, one of his Jewish captives, and one of God's great servants of all time, who gave to Nebuchadnezzar the divine interpretation of his unusual dream, in which he saw "the times of the Gentiles" represented by "a great [human] image of excellent brightness and terrible form" (that is, terrifying in its appearance).

3. *The course of "the times of the Gentiles."* The important point to note here is that there is an unbroken *decrease in value,* accompanied by a steady *increase in strength,* of the four metals of the image: gold to silver to brass to iron. This would seem to foretell clearly just what history has recorded: internal (moral and spiritual) deterioration despite apparent progress in the realm of the external.

4. *The identity of "the times of the Gentiles."* Through Daniel, God specifically identifies the Gentile world powers as

represented by this great image, and history has faithfully recorded an exact fulfillment of the sure Word of prophecy, as it ever does. From head of gold to feet and toes of iron and clay, there are four, and only four, Gentile powers to hold world-wide sway. Babylon is first; followed by Media-Persia; then Greece; and, finally, Rome. This prophecy alone has been, and is, more than sufficient to preclude utterly the possibility of any other Gentile nation becoming mistress of the world. That is for us extremely enlightening and wonderfully comforting.

5. *The nature of the "times of the Gentiles."* But Nebuchadnezzar's dream-image tells only half of the story, depicting, as it does, the *apparent* greatness and majesty of "the times of the Gentiles" *from man's viewpoint.* Some years later the prophet Daniel had a great prophetic dream also, and he beholds the Gentile powers in their true nature, as seen by the omniscient God. This time there is no great imposing image; but rather, a succession of cruel, ravenous beasts, becoming ever more ferocious. From the lion (Babylon) to the great and terrible non-descript beast (Rome), the sway of Gentile dominion has been increasingly ruthless and bestial. Thus have the blood-drenched battlefields of the world down through the centuries borne eloquent testimony to the wonderful accuracy of the prophetic Word. The reason for this is that the Gentiles have no more sought to rule *for* God than did disobedient Israel; and if He be not honored, Satan, the destroyer, will inevitably hold sway. Thus it has been, and is even today, with all the evils and horrors that must accompany satanic rulership in the councils of the nations.

6. *The final form of "the times of the Gentiles."* It is to be recalled that the four successive Gentile world powers are foretold by the image of Daniel 2 and the beasts of Daniel 7. The fourth one is Rome, and a study of these chapters clearly shows that it is this one which will hold world-wide dominion in the end of this age, to be overthrown and destroyed by

Christ when He comes to terminate the wicked era of "the times of the Gentiles" and set up His glorious millennial kingdom on earth. But, one might ask, has not Rome already had her time of world rulership? The answer is that she has partially but not completely run her alloted course. In its entirety, Rome's time is depicted by the legs of iron and feet and toes of iron and clay (Daniel 2:40-43), and by the great non-descript beast of Daniel 7:7, 8.

Following the crucifixion of Christ, in which she played such a leading role as the Gentile world empire, Rome's dominion was eventually broken, leaving the "feet and toes" of the image, and the "ten horns" of the beast yet to be fulfilled. In other words, she has been "wounded, as it were, to death," but "the deadly wound is to be healed": she is to be revived as a world empire for a brief season to receive her just punishment for the role she played at Calvary. This is as logical as it is clear: the prophetic Word is specific in saying that the pulverizing blow to the image of Daniel 2 will be dealt to its *feet and toes* by the returning King of kings who will then set up His supreme, universal kingdom; and who should He more fittingly overthrow than the proud Rome which sentenced Him to death?

But what is to be Rome's final (revived) form? The answer is found in the "feet and toes," and in the "ten horns." The original Roman Empire, as depicted by the "legs of iron" of the image, was made up of two divisions (Eastern and Western) when it eventually fell, and, in its future and final revived form, the "legs of iron" quite naturally merge into the "feet and toes of iron and clay." The "ten toes" of Daniel 2 and the "ten horns" of Daniel 7 both speak of the fact that Rome revived will be a ten-nation federation holding world-wide dominion in the general sphere formerly occupied by Rome when she ruled the whole world. And, while we would not be dogmatic about this, it would seem logical to conclude that, inasmuch as five toes are on each foot, five of these nations will occupy the old Eastern division and five the Western.

At this point, attention is called to the fact that, when she formerly ruled the world, Rome's sphere, generally speaking, was in the territory surrounding the Mediterranean: from the British Isles to the Euphrates, and from North Africa to the Rhine and Danube. Again we eschew dogmatism, but a logical interpretation of the sure Word of prophecy would seem to demand that Rome revived should essentially occupy about this same sphere (and also include America and the other English-speaking countries which have sprung from Britain).

Out of the recent world wars, and in the midst of world-shaking events transpiring today in the family of nations, we might well ask: Are there indications that Rome is preparing herself for the vital role she is to play in the great end-time drama? We verily believe so, and in a most startling manner, as is evidenced by the way the Western democracies are being welded into an integrated federation of nations by the threat of Red Russia. And these democracies almost completely coincide with the geographical boundaries of ancient Rome!

But what of the fact that Rome (Italy) today shows no particular promise of suddenly becoming mistress of the world? The first answer to this question is to let it be a solemn warning against "date-setting" or "prophesying" on our part. Another answer is found in the fact that great and unexpected changes take place in the affairs of the nations almost overnight. (To grasp the truth of this, one has only to compare the status and alignment of nations today with that of five or ten years ago, or even less.) But we believe the specific answer to this question is found in Daniel 9:26, where *the* Antichrist, the coming great world dictator, is to be a *Roman*. He is seen arising as the dominating "horn" among the other "ten horns" of Daniel 7:7, 8, and, being satanically empowered, there is no reason to doubt his supernatural ability suddenly and dramatically to raise himself and his Roman Empire to world dominion, when that moment strikes after the Rapture of the Church.

7. *The doom of "the times of the Gentiles."* How tragically has Satan deluded the proud Gentile nations into thinking that they, and not God, will have the last word! When the image is finally complete; when the beast is apparently invincible; when *the* Antichrist rules unchallenged, without regard for God or man; then comes the final, crushing blow as the King of kings triumphantly returns in great power and glory to put down all rule, and establish His kingdom in all the earth. Christ, the Stone which the builders rejected, "smites the image upon his feet and breaks it in pieces which shall be carried away like the chaff of the summer threshingfloors." Then, and only then, do the kingdoms of this world become the kingdoms of Christ, their rightful Sovereign.

Chapter XXII

THE ASSEMBLING OF THE CAST: RUSSIA

As "the day of Jacob's trouble" (the consummation of the age) draws nigh, the spotlight of prophecy turns toward the north, whence Israel's dreaded enemies so often swooped down upon her in times past. But these assaults, despite their fury and ferocity, were but faint foreshadows of the great northern army and its merciless invasion of Palestine predicted for the end-time by Ezekiel 38 and 39, and Joel 2. Thus does the inerrant Word of prophecy cast its all-revealing rays upon *Russia,* that sinister nation which is so persistently in the limelight at the present time.

1. *Her identification.* "The chief prince" of Ezekiel 38:2 is literally and correctly translated "the Prince of Rosh." Thus "Gog" is the "Prince of Rosh, Meshech and Tubal," while "Magog" is his land. That "Rosh, Meshech and Tubal" at once suggest Russia, Moscow and Tobolsk is too patent to be denied, and this is abundantly confirmed by the findings of

103

able and learned ethnologists and geographers whose testimony is irresistible that Russia is the subject of the prophecy of Ezekiel 38 and 39. (A few quotations will suffice to substantiate this interpretation: "The Scythians [progenitors of the modern Russians] were called by the Greeks, Magog," according to Josephus the noted Jewish historian. "As early as the ninth century A.D., the Danes or Northmen were called 'the people of Gog and Magog,'" according to another authority; and, finally, we cite the following from a learned and sober interpreter of prophecy, Bishop Lowth: "Rosh, taken as a proper name in Ezekiel, signifies the inhabitants of Scythia, from whom the modern Russians derive their name.") And, if further verification of Russia's identity be needed, Ezekiel 38:15; Ezekiel 39:1, 2; and Joel 2:20 would seem to furnish irrefutable proof by specifically locating this great end-time enemy of God and Israel as coming out of the *north*.

2. *Her time.* "After many days" (from the time of Ezekiel's prophecy); "in the latter years" (the end-time of the age); and "into the land brought back from the sword, gathered out of many people, against the mountains of Israel, which have been waste: but it is brought forth out of the nations, and they shall dwell safely." Here, it seems, is a threefold declaration of the time when Russia will play her role, and it points to the consummation of the age when Israel will be back in Palestine, still generally rejecting the Messiah, but dwelling in *apparent* safety.

We use the word "apparent" advisedly, and by no means dogmatically, because worthy and devout Bible scholars are not agreed as to just when Russia's attack on Palestine will take place. We are inclined to believe that Russia will attack Israel during the seven-year age-ending Tribulation and *before* Christ returns in glorious power.

In the first place, it seems to us that reference to "the latter years" puts this attack in the end-time of this age, and not in the beginning of Christ's reign. Then, as to Israel's dwelling in *safety*, it is our belief that this is somehow related to Daniel 9:27 which speaks of the "covenant" that Antichrist makes with Israel for seven years. Exactly what the covenant is we cannot know, but it is reasonable to believe that it must contain some guarantee of safety and security to Israel against attack, in return perhaps for exclusive access to the abundant natural resources now being discovered in Palestine. Revelation 6:1, 2 confirms the fact that Antichrist dupes the world into falling at his feet by offering an apparent cure for war, and Israel might well be a prime beneficiary (to her way of thinking) of this great dictator.

Then, by comparing Revelation 6:1-4 with I Thessalonians 5:1-2, we get a graphic picture of an unprecedented war engulfing the sadly deluded world, which had been made to think that the Antichrist had actually brought in millennial peace.

The second chapter of Joel indicates rather definitely that the northern army invades Israel during the early or middle part of the seven-year Tribulation; and Ezekiel 38:13 suggests that Russia and her hordes are challenged by the revived Roman Empire of the Antichrist. It would therefore not seem impossible that the attack by Russia on Palestine *might* precipitate the terrible holocaust of Revelation 6:3, 4, after which the Antichrist holds unchallenged sway over all the world until he is destroyed by Christ at His return.

3. *Her Policy*. Ezekiel 38:7 is another illustration of the exquisite accuracy of the Word of prophecy. Centuries ago it was foretold that Russia would gain her allies by craftily swallowing them up under the pretense of "guarding" them. Today we see this very thing happening as she overcomes one defenseless people after another in the assumed role of "protector"!

4. *Her allies*. The allies include Persia (modern Iran); Ethiopia and Libya (maybe the Ethiopia of Eastern Africa and the Libya of Northern Africa, but more likely Arabian

countries formerly of these names in the old Babylonian territory of the Middle East); Gomer (definitely identifiable with Germany, and evidently the Eastern part of Germany, lying out of the sphere of the revived Roman Empire); Togarmah (ancient Armenia, presently absorbed by Russia and Turkey); and "many people with thee" (the Far Eastern hordes?). The only comment needed here is to suggest the reading of the daily newspaper in the light of these prophecies. Their significance today is inescapable.

5. *Her goal.* What prompts Russia to attack Palestine? The Word of prophecy says that her evil intention is to take a spoil from the nation (Israel) "dwelling in the land of unwalled villages" (Palestine). It is common knowledge that Russia is greatly lacking in oil and other vital natural resources, and she will not be satisfied even after swallowing up her predicted allies. She will cast a greedy eye towards defenseless Palestine which has recently been called "an engineer's paradise" because of the continuing discoveries of almost illimitable wealth in the Dead Sea and other areas.

6. *Her enemies.* If our interpretation be correct, that Russia will probably attack Palestine during the seven-year, age-ending tribulation period, then Ezekiel 38:13 would seem to confirm our belief that she will be challenged by the revived Roman Empire under the Antichrist. The consensus seems to be that Tarshish refers to Britain; and "all the young lions thereof" to America and other English-speaking countries which we believe will form a most vital part of the revived Empire. Some think that the language of this verse indicates only a diplomatic protest on the part of the Western Empire, and no military action; their view being that Russia's downfall is brought about by God's supernatural intervention. That this may possibly be the correct interpretation we do not for a moment deny; but, at the same time, we are inclined to think that the language here is figurative, and that there will be warfare in a very real sense. However, this does not mean

that Russia is defeated purely by human means; on the contrary, the latter part of Ezekiel 38 and 39 seems to indicate clearly that the God of the universe unleashes the fury of nature on His implacable foe with such devastating force that but a sixth part of the once-mighty horde is left.

7. *Her defeat.* Anti-God, anti-Christ and anti-Israel, Russia's doom is inevitable. Whether directly, or through human instrumentality, or both, Ezekiel's great prophecy makes it abundantly clear that, in due time, she will feel the consuming wrath of God. God says He is against her. Why? Because she is unalterably and viciously opposed to God, as evidenced by her salute (the raised clenched fist); by her actions; and by her own statements: "We will grapple with the Lord God in due season. We shall vanquish Him in His highest heaven, and wherever He seeks refuge, and we shall subdue Him forever." Little wonder that her doom is both sealed and terrible.

Chapter XXIII

THE ASSEMBLING OF THE CAST: ISRAEL

OUTLINE FOR CHAPTER XXIII

The budding of the fig tree (see Matt. 24:32, 33).
1. Israel's regathering to the Promised land: Zeph. 2:1, 2.
    a. Revival of the nation: Is. 43:5, 6; Jer. 33:7; Ezek. 37.
    b. Revival of the land: Is. 43:19, 20; 51:3; Ezek. 36:7-11,
       30, 35.
    c. Revival of the language: Zeph. 3:9a.
2. Israel's chastisement in the end-days (preceding her regeneration and
   glorification): Jer. 30:1-7.
    a. Punished by the Lord: Jer. 30:1-7; Amos 3:1, 2; Jer. 11:17;
       Hos. 9:9; 12:2.
    b. Scourged by the northern army: Ezek. 38:10-12; Joel
       2:1-10, 20.
    c. Tormented by Satan: Dan. 9:27; Matt. 24:15-22; Rev. 12.
    d. The vortex of Armageddon: Dan. 12:1; Joel 3:1, 2, 9-16;
       Zech. 12:1-3; 14:1, 2.

Note: See Appendix I, Definitions 5, 16, 22 and 26.

If, as is true, Palestine be the center of the world stage,
then surely Israel, the chosen people, is the central figure in
the coming end-time drama. This is confirmed by the fact
that, according to the sure Word of prophecy, "the consummation of the age" is actually "the day of Jacob's trouble."

Consequently, of all the multiplied indications heralding the
fast-approaching consummation of the age, it is our firm con-
viction that Israel is *the key sign;* so that if she, "God's fig
tree," definitely begins to bud (showing signs of reviving as
a nation *in her land*), then may we indeed know that He is
near, "even at the doors."

1. *Israel's regathering to the Promised Land.* These important verses (Zeph. 2:1, 2) point out a very significant truth: Israel gathers herself together (mostly in unbelief and continued rejection of Jesus as the Messiah) *before* the end-time tribulation. Which is to say that, although she is marvelously helped of the Lord in this partial and preliminary regathering, the regathering *precedes* her final and complete restoration to the Holy Land as a purged and regenerated nation at the return of the Christ whom she will then accept. Thus does "Jacob" (unwittingly) return to Palestine for the "day of his trouble" — the consummation of the age which is so significantly heralded by Israel's regathering. We shall now briefly consider a threefold sign of the budding of the fig tree.

a. *Revival of the nation.* The meaning here is national revival in a political, and not a spiritual sense. On this vital topic there is no more important passage than Ezekiel 37 which contains the prophet's unusual vision of the valley of dry bones. This is explained to be a picture of the chosen nation dead as such — scattered among all the nations of the world upon her rejection and crucifixion of Messiah. In this dispersed condition there seems to be little hope for national life again. But, the Almighty One begins to act and the dry bones *do* live: Israel's restoration to life *as a nation in her land* is guaranteed. Further, let it be carefully noted that this marvelous prophecy is in Ezekiel 37, just preceding the account in chapters 38 and 39 of the coming vicious attack on restored Israel in Palestine, by Russia and her hordes, during the end-time period of "Jacob."

And now we raise the vital question: Are there signs of the budding of the fig tree? The answer is obvious. While there were only some 50,000 Jews in Palestine after World War I, there are today (in 1954) over 2,000,000! On May 14, 1948, Israel was *officially* reborn as a nation! This stupendous fact is alone sufficient to satisfy the honest seeker that the consummation of the age is very nigh; but when viewed in the light of the numerous other sure heralds of its nearness, the proof is overwhelming that the return of Christ must indeed be imminent, especially when it is remembered that, in the case of the fig tree, there is only a brief time between the budding and the fruit. (And of utmost significance to the born-again Christian is the promise of our Lord to come for us even *before* the end-time drama begins!)

b. *Revival of the land.* Simultaneous with the revival of the chosen people as a nation in Palestine, God has promised to begin the restoration of her desolated land to its Eden-like state of beauty and fruitfulness. The people and the land are inseparable in God's program: when Israel was scattered among the nations of the world, Palestine was made a waste and desolate, a barren and desert land. But now Israel is back in the Promised Land and, as He had promised, He has begun to "make a way in the wilderness, and rivers in the desert" (Is. 43:19). What a thrilling commentary do we have here on the sure Word of prophecy!

Not many decades ago a delegation was sent to Palestine to investigate its possibilities as a suitable homeland for scattered Israel, but they reported the land as being too desolate to take care of the people. Today it would be difficult, if not impossible, to find a more flourishing, fruitful and fast-growing country than the Palestine of Israel! Hath He spoken, and will He not do it? He promised to restore His people to their land, and, at the same time, restore the land for His people; thus before our very eyes we behold a veritable miracle as the great Creator opens up springs in the desert, makes the wilderness flourish, and the desert to blossom like the rose! The fact that this restoration of the land is only partial and preliminary, its final and complete fruition coming at the return of Christ, in no wise minimizes the significance and import of the wonderful fulfillment of prophecy we are witnessing *today*.

c. *Revival of the language.* The Jews having returned from

more than seventy nations, it would seem that there would be an acute language problem in the new-born nation, Israel. But, true to His sure Word of prophecy, their God has begun marvelously to "turn the people to a pure language" — the ancient Hebrew of their fathers (and the holy language of the Old Testament). It is now the official language of Israel, and is spoken by more than ninety per cent of the Jews in Palestine, although they have come from the four corners of the earth! The people, the land, the language — all being wonderfully and simultaneously revived exactly as foretold in the prophetic Word!

2. *The day of Jacob's trouble.* But before her glorious destiny is realized and manifested to the world, the suffering nation must go through her greatest hour of trial as she plays the most tragic role in the end-time tragedy. Except for the inerrant truth of the Word of prophecy, it would seem hard to believe that Israel's persecution could exceed that which she has suffered down through the centuries at the hands of the Pharaohs, Hamans and Hitlers, but "there shall be a time of trouble, such as never was since there was a nation," so terrible that Michael the great archangel must needs stand in the gap for the chosen people (Dan. 12:1).

a. *Punished by the Lord.* This is essentially the root cause of Jacob's coming day of trouble. Much-beloved, but persistently disobedient, the Christ-rejecting nation must feel the wrath of her holy God. The very fact that the seven-year tribulation period seems to be initiated by a solemn treaty between Israel and *the* Antichrist is sufficient to account for the great outpouring of God's righteous anger during those terrible days.

b. *Scourged by the northern army.* The Lord God will, as heretofore, also use human instruments in His scourging of His wandering people. And, as in olden times, one of Israel's most feared and cruel persecutors will again swoop down from the north to burn and sear the Holy Land in indescribable fury.

c. *Tormented by Satan.* Archenemy of God and God's people, the Devil will be *personally* on the earth during the last three and one-half years (the most intense part) of the seven-year Tribulation. Knowing that his time is now short, the old destroyer looses all his supernatural hate and fury against the chosen nation, through whom Christ came the first time, and through whom He is yet to manifest all His glorious power and authority earthward. Revelation 12 graphically describes this all-out assault on Israel, and her deliverance by the hand of her God, who will not let even Satan exterminate the indestructible nation, for He has a purpose which cannot be thwarted: and the chosen people are central in His program.

d. *The vortex of Armageddon.* As the horrible Tribulation roars toward its awful climax, with Satan personally on earth, his Antichrist on the world-throne, and the False Prophet (the religious counterpart of Antichrist) holding sway in Jerusalem, all the nations of the earth join in sending their mighty armies into Palestine to wipe out the last vestige of God, God's people and God's city, Jerusalem. Just as the trinity of evil seems to have victory in its grasp, the mighty Christ flashes forth from heaven in irresistible power to destroy these evil forces and deliver His People from their most agonizing hour. Thus does disobedient Israel drink the cup of God's wrath to the last drop — even to the point of apparent destruction and extermination in the last and greatest battle of a war-seared age. But, as specifically foretold by Daniel (12:1), the purged, believing, regenerated remnant is gloriously delivered to enter Christ's blessed kingdom on earth as the ruling and honored nation.

Chapter XXIV

THE ASSEMBLING OF THE CAST: THE COUNTERFEIT CHURCH

Satan's most successful efforts to keep man from God have ever been those of imitation, half-truths and counterfeits. And, as the end-time tragedy approaches, we see him exercising all his diabolical cunning and craftiness as he prepares his masterpieces for their coming roles: a Counterfeit Christ, a Counterfeit World Empire, a Counterfeit Israel and a Counterfeit Church. It is this latter personage to whom our thoughts now reluctantly turn.

1. *Its growth and development.* There is good reason to

113

doubt that a single verse of Scripture has been more grossly and universally misinterpreted than Matthew 12:33, which has been completely twisted to mean that the Church is to convert the whole world (in the absence of the King) by the preaching of the "leaven of the Gospel." This is the very opposite of the correct interpretation — that the "leaven" of sin and evil has been working its corrupt work in the realm of Christendom from the beginning and will eventually leaven "the whole." If this verse be read with ordinary care, and in the light of the context and of other Scriptures on the subject of leaven, the correct meaning is made abundantly clear. The whole burden of Matthew 13 is the evil nature and course of this wicked age during the absence of the King; that is, a picture of the kingdom of heaven while the King is, as it were, forcibly denied His rightful rulership. The first parable sets the pattern by clearly showing that even all who hear the Gospel will not believe; while the second shows that the tares (children of Satan) are persistently and increasingly found intermingled with the wheat (the children of God), so much so that the age must end in judgment. This judgment-ending is also clearly depicted by the last parable — the dragnet. The fifth mystery ("the hid treasure") is a picture of the chosen nation, Israel, scattered among the nations of the world, apparently dead and buried there nationally, but preserved by the God who loves her. The sixth mystery ("the pearl") has previously been shown to be the true Church for which Christ gave all.

Invariably "leaven" in the Holy Scriptures has an evil connotation. This can be readily proved by checking all of its occurrences, beginning with Exodus 12:15 and ending with Galatians 5:9. (Here the question might be raised as to Leviticus 23:17, where God directs Israel to bake the wave-loaves with leaven; but when it is noted that the feast at which these were offered was a type of Pentecost, the birthday of the Church, it will easily be seen that this by no means contradicts, but definitely confirms the teaching of Matthew 13:33 that the leaven of sin has done its corrupting work in Christendom from the beginning.)

Christ warned against "leaven," and Paul likewise (I Cor. 5:6-8). Could it be possible for them to warn against the precious Gospel? Assuredly not. The prophetic Scriptures are one in saying that this present evil age gets worse and worse and ends in judgment; history abundantly sets its seal on this truth; logic and reason demand that the millennial kingdom be not set up until the rightful King of kings returns. These all constitute overwhelming proof that Matthew 13:33 can only mean that Satan has been internally corrupting Christendom with the "leaven" of sin from the beginning, and will yet "leaven the whole."

From the loss of first love in the apostolic period to complete apostasy in the final, Laodicean stage, the leaven of corruption has indeed done its insidious work, a work which can only result in the "whole being leavened." The continued presence on earth of the true Church (the "salt") acts to prevent the final and complete corruption that must lead to judgment; but when the Bride of Church is raptured, the counterfeit church will rapidly assume and manifest its real character, and will play its important role in the end-time tragedy.

2. *Its final form.* We return briefly to Matthew 13, and in verses 31 and 32 find the counterfeit church full-bloomed: a great, unnatural tree, grown from the tiny mustard seed, and giving lodging to the birds of the air (Rev. 18:2 confirms the evil character of this monstrosity). This is the final outworking of the leaven of corruption, the ultimate outcome of the loss of first love, worldliness, idolatry, formalism and apostasy. This religious "Babylon" (of utter confusion, deception and evil) is portrayed in detail in Revelation 17 and 18.

a. *The outward appearance.* Rich, powerful and seductively beautiful does she appear to the nations of the earth as she allures men with her ritualistic appeal to their religious yearnings, and as she fascinates them with her offer of glory and prestige, and the pleasures of sin without its inevitable consequences. Hers is, in short, "an easy religion," saying, in effect, that the poor deluded sinner may expect salvation through her powerful mediation even though he cling to all his sin. And thousands, yea millions, are the willing victims of this "scarlet woman," because she exercises her satanic sway under the guise of "religion." To be sure, there is "a form of Godliness"; otherwise, it would not really be a *counterfeit*. And Satan is a pastmaster at the art of imitation, as is strikingly evidenced as we consider Apostate Christendom even today, before it assumes its final evil form.

There is much lip service, but little heart love for God and Christ and the Word; much sanctimonious, but meaningless oratory; awe-inspiring, but dead ritual; magnificent, but sepulchral edifices; superlative, but lifeless organization; a high-sounding, but earthly and unscriptural program; self-righteous, pompous, but twice-dead leaders; limitless material wealth and temporal influence and power, but Spiritual poverty; in short, "having a form of Godliness, but denying the power thereof."

This, we submit, is the world church of the end-time, as she will appear when idolatrous Rome and apostate Protestantism emerge, united, as the counterfeit church after the Rapture of the Bride of Christ. We believe the language of Revelation 17 and 18 indicates Rome will play the leading role in this, which would be entirely consistent both with her world-wide and powerful organization, and with her avowed claim that her head, the Pope, is the present vice-regent of Christ on earth. Neither she nor apostate Christendom are the least averse to undertaking the setting up of the millennial kingdom in the absence of the King of kings. Rather is that their aim, and this is clearly evidenced by the fact that this all-powerful counterfeit church is instrumental in the rise of the Antichrist to world power, and surely also a vital factor in the coming revival of the old Roman Empire.

b. *The real nature.* To man this "woman upon a scarlet beast" is fascinatingly beautiful and alluring; but God looks beneath the surface and sees that "her golden cup is full of abominations and filthiness." She, the great religious leader of the world, is actually "drunken with the blood of the saints" she has martyred because they refused her the allegiance and homage due only to the Lord Jesus Christ. Great is her responsibility, and great is her condemnation — "her sins reach to heaven," so persistently and willfully has she trespassed against the light.

3. *Its doom.* Seduced by the world, married to the world, dominating the world and, finally, destroyed by the world — that is, briefly, the tragic story of Christ — rejecting, apostate Christendom. The counterfeit church evidently reaches the zenith of her power in the end-time, after the true Church has been raptured, and, for a brief time, enjoys her role as mistress of the nations, being, as it were, "the power behind the throne." But after Satan is cast down personally to the earth in the midst of the seven-year Tribulation, even this blasphemous pretense to religion is too much for him to permit and so the counterfeit church meets her sudden, unexpected and complete destruction at the hands of her erstwhile companion, Antichrist, and his confederates. This is God's answer to apostate Christendom: "I will spue thee out of my mouth."

Chapter XXV

THE ASSEMBLING OF THE CAST: SATAN

118

4. Satan vs. God: Is. 14:13, 14; Zech. 3:1, 2; II Thess. 2:4, 9.
   a. Adversary of Christ at His first advent: Luke 4:1-13; John 14:30.
   b. Makes desperate effort to retain permanent control of the kingdoms of this world after being cast down to the earth during Tribulation: Rev. 12:7-12; 16:13-16.
   c. Conquered and bound by Christ at His glorious return: Rev. 20:1-3.
   d. Makes final all-out effort against God at close of Millenium: Rev. 20:7-9a.
5. Satan's eternal doom: Rev. 20:9b, 10.
Note: See Appendix I, Definitions 21, 22 and 32.

We conclude our preview of the cast with a brief glimpse of the villain himself, none other than Satan, who is also known as the Devil, the Serpent and the Destroyer. Although he is unwillingly on the stage in person during the final act (the last three and one half of the seven years), he is essentially the one "behind the scenes, directing and controlling his puppets as they perform their heinous end-time roles."

1. *Satan's origin.* A most important illustration of the need ever to divide the Word of truth rightly is found in Ezekiel 28, where the message, beginning at verse 12, is directed no longer toward the King of Tyre, but to Satan. This invaluable passage contains the comforting assurance that the one we rightly call the Devil, is, after all, only creature and not *Creator,* despite the fact that he undeniably has supernatural powers. That he was originally at the top of the created order, "full of wisdom" and "perfect in beauty," cannot be gainsaid. And verse 13 seems to indicate definitely that the Garden of Eden on this planet was his home and headquarters as he exercised his authority and carried out his duties somewhat as God's "prime minister."

2. *Satan's fall.* In Isaiah 14 we see him (Lucifer, the son of the morning) as, in some mysterious way that we cannot fathom, sin was suddenly born in his heart; and this first mani-

festation of sin was in the form of pride. Lucifer, through the pronouncement of his five "I wills," proclaimed his independence of, and rebellion against the God of the universe. Thus was sin born, and this was doubtless the moment when "Satan, as lightning, fell from heaven," because the Almighty One must alone be sovereign and supreme.

Attending his fall was the similar downfall of a host of angels, those who chose to follow Lucifer in his awful rebellion against their Maker and Master.

And there seems to be strong evidence that our earth was victimized by this inestimable tragedy, for we are told in Genesis 1:2 that "the earth *became* waste and void." We know that a perfect God could not have created the earth thus, and this is specifically asserted in Isaiah 45:18. So this planet must have undergone some horrible catastrophe after its original perfect creation as told in Genesis 1:1. Since Ezekiel clearly indicates that Lucifer dwelt in the Garden of Eden before he fell, the conclusion seems obvious that we have here the correct explanation of the laying waste of the earth, which is perhaps described in Isaiah 24:1.

3. *Satan vs. humanity*. In the light of the foregoing we are better prepared to understand what took place in the tragic chapter of Genesis 3. There can be little doubt that Satan looked on in bitter envy and rising fury as God restored the earth to its Edenic perfection and beauty, and put thereon another to enjoy its blessedness, even man. So perhaps very little time elapsed before the Subtle One, in the guise of the beautiful serpent (which it was then), appeared to Eve, seduced her to doubt God's Word, enticed her to eat of the forbidden fruit (following his example of rebellion against God), and thus injected the deadly virus of sin into the newly created human race.

The battle of the ages was joined, between Satan and man, and it continues to rage unabated. Above all else, the Devil's aim has been to deprive his victim of a way of salvation from the curse and penalty of sin. And so when the Saviour (the Seed of the woman, Gen. 3:15) came the first time, the old Serpent viciously sought to get man to destroy his only hope of redemption. He apparently succeeded, but the Almighty One turned apparent defeat into supreme triumph, bringing forth His Beloved Son from the grave, and offering to sinners everywhere a sure escape from the clutches of Satan and sin through faith in the shed blood of the Lord Jesus Christ.

However, the fact remained that, generally speaking, the human race said "no" to God at Calvary and refused His Son, who returned to heaven after His resurrection, leaving Satan, by man's choice, as the god of this age. And thus it is that throughout these wicked days "we wrestle not against flesh and blood, but against principalities, against powers, against world rulers of this darkness, against spiritual wickedness in the heavenlies." Which is to say, "Satan is the prince of the power of the air," whence he directs his wiles against mankind, as he holds tyrannical sway over his kingdom of demons.

What a great and terrible adversary is ours! The Accuser, the Destroyer, the Deceiver, the Roaring Lion, the Prince of Death itself. "But thanks be unto God who giveth us the victory through our Lord Jesus Christ." The tragedy is that, as an angel of light, this archenemy of man increasingly conquers millions upon millions through his cunning and deceit, so that he would literally win the final victory in the war of the ages were it not for Him who alone is more powerful, our blessed Redeemer.

4. *Satan vs. God.* But his warfare against humanity is really only incidental to his unrelenting battle against God, and especially against the Christ of God. First he tried unsuccessfully to deflect our Lord from Calvary by tempting Him to accept the kingdoms of the world from him who had usurped them through sin. Failing here, he tried to destroy Christ through death, but actually sealed his own ultimate doom, as

our Lord, through death, conquered Satan, sin and death for us.

Presently, the Devil is enjoying his day of apparent victory, being, by man's choice, the ruler of this age. But the stage and the cast are rapidly being prepared for the certain defeat of God's great enemy, even though he shall, at the climax of the Tribulation, gather all the armies of his subservient world together against the Lord and His Christ. However, the gloriously returning King of kings will seize and securely bind the Serpent when He comes back to take over the rightful rulership of the world, so that, during His blessed millennial reign, the nations will no more be deceived by him who is properly called the great Deceiver.

And this would appear to be the final crushing of the head of the Serpent to end the conflict of the ages; but the end is not yet. For, at the close of Christ's thousand-year reign, Satan is loosed for a final brief season, and he leads an innumerable host in a last all-out attack against God. This not only proves the inveterate evil of the unregenerated human heart, but also serves to demonstrate clearly the irremedial rebellion and wickedness of Satan himself. He has declared war to the end against God, and thus it shall be. There is no vestige of any basis for compromise or agreement in the least; there is no iota of common ground for God and Satan, Righteousness and Sin, Light and Darkness, Life and Death, Good and Evil.

5. *Satan's eternal doom*. Suddenly the omnipotent God roars from heaven in His righteous anger, and it is all over. The Evil One is overcome, and cast into the "lake of fire and brimstone," the awful and eternal abiding place not only for him, but for all his followers in rebellion against God, whether angels or men.

Chapter XXVI

THE SOUNDING OF THE PRELUDE

There remains to be discussed the specific question as asked by the disciples in Matthew 24:3: What is *the* sign of the consummation of the age? (not "end of the world" as erroneously translated). This plain inquiry definitely assumes that there will be an unmistakable sign specifically heralding the end, in addition to the somewhat general signs we have already considered. And, taken together, these would afford the believer a solid foundation upon which to build his hopes of the Lord's early return.

Several factors confirm this as the proper interpretation. In the first place, our Lord did not rebuke the disciples for seeking such information; rather he warned them against deception and thus clearly implied that there would be such a sign and exhorted them to discern it spiritually. Then, we have been told that the Day of the Lord is not to overtake us as a thief because we are children of light and not darkness, (I Thess. 5:4, 5), which clearly implies that we are to be aware of its nearness. Again, the Lord severely rebuked the Scribes and Pharisees for willfully shutting their eyes to the multiplied signs of His first advent: and if that be so, how much more should we, His children, be aware of the import and meaning of all the heralds of His return? And, finally, after answering the question of the disciples, He not only permits but commands them to *know* that he is near, "even at the doors," when they see all these foretold things coming to pass.

Then, knowing the tendency of the human mind and heart to go beyond that which is written, our omniscient Lord, in Matthew 24:36, rings out a clear and unmistakable warning: "But of that day and hour, knoweth no man." And we wholeheartedly bow to this admonition of our blessed Lord against any and all "datesetting." But there still remains the "know that He is near" of verse 33. The divine, perfect Christ does not mock: would He tell us in one breath to know by certain signs that He is near, and then in the next say that we must not and cannot know it? The answer is obvious: We are clearly enjoined to know that He is near, but strictly warned against trying to set the exact time.

At this point it might be helpful to observe once again the exquisite accuracy of the Word, and the great importance of rightly dividing it at all times. In this case, our Lord uses, on the one hand, the word "near," as against "day and hour" on the other. It can be readily seen that here is a fine and delicate distinction designed to convey perfectly the intended message and impression: for our comfort, inspiration and edification He wants us to *know* that His return is *near;* but He warns us against stepping over the line and indulging in the forbidden pastime of hurtful, destructive and sinful "datesetting."

It is important, also, to note the part that the believer's attitude plays in this vital matter. To point this up, let us ask the frank question: Just why do I want to know about the signs indicating His near return? If we can sincerely answer: For my comfort, inspiration, and edification, so that I may love Him more and seek lost men more zealously while it is still the day of salvation, and be found ready when He does come; then we fully believe this is His gracious message to such a guileless, earnest believer. But if on the other hand, the motive be not pure, if morbid curiosity, sensation seeking, or any other unlawful and sinful desire be at the root of the study of prophecy, and particularly this phase of it, then we verily believe Christ's solemn warning applies in all its force.

Eschewing any and all complicity with this evil practice of attempting to set dates, we now ask: What shall be *the* sign of the consummation of the age?

1. *A definite sign.* After warning the disciples against being deceived by false Christs, our Lord proceeds to tell them what the sign is by first telling them what it is *not*. False Christs, wars and rumors of wars, are to characterize the whole course of "this present evil age," and, in themselves, are not the sign. History has amply verified this with its blood-stained record of the countless wars down through the centuries since the Prince of Peace was rejected and slain.

Then, in verses 7 and 8, the omniscient Christ specifies that which shall constitute *the* sign (literally, "the beginning of travail"): Nation against nation, and kingdom against kingdom (war on a world-wide scale between kingdoms, or federations, of nations), followed by famines, and pestilences, and earthquakes."

2. *A universal sign.* This feature is again mentioned to emphasize its importance. The sign is to be a *world-wide* war, followed by famines, pestilences and earthquakes on a world-wide scale ("in divers places").

3. *A composite sign.* For a world-wide war to be the sign of the end, it must be accompanied and followed by famines, pestilences and earthquakes on a world-wide scale. In other

words, all the essential ingredients must coexist before the sign can be labelled genuine.

4. *A confirmed sign.* After briefly describing the sign of the end in verses 7 and 8, our Lord, beginning with verse 9 and continuing through verse 31, proceeds to picture what the awful seven-year Tribulation will be like when it actually arrives. At verse 32 He returns to the answer concerning the sign of the end, and cites an additional factor, the presence of which will serve to doubly confirm the definite, universal and composite sign of world-wide warfare, famines, pestilences and earthquakes. And it seems to us that our Lord is here saying: When you see all these things, accompanied and followed by the budding of the fig tree, (*Israel's national revival in Palestine*), then may you indeed know that I am near, even at the doors.

5. *A sure sign.* The sign is definite, universal, composite, confirmed and certain — guaranteed by the sure Word of prophecy which will stand even though heaven and earth pass away. God is not man that He should either lie or change. And He has condescended to tell us how we may *know* that it is near. Surely we may as fully trust His immutable Word here as elsewhere!

But what is the significance of verse 34? "Verily I say unto you, This generation shall not pass, till all these things be fulfilled." There is no difficulty about "all these things"; they doubtless refer to the seven-year age-ending Tribulation and the coming glory of Christ at its end to establish His millennial kingdom. But to what does our Lord have reference when He says, *"This generation shall not pass* till all these things be fulfilled"? There are two possible interpretations, and each is supported by able and consecrated men of God, so we feel that dogmatism in either direction is most certainly not warranted.

There are those who hold that "this generation" means Israel, the chosen race, and that our Lord is here confirming the multiplied promises of the Old Testament that she will be preserved for her leading role in the millennial kingdom despite all the efforts of Satan and men to destroy her. This interpretation is sound, and the reasoning logical: for Israel might well despair of coming through such an ordeal as the "day of Jacob's trouble." But she has His assurance that a purged, believing remnant will be preserved through it all.

On the other hand, there are those who believe that, consistent with the time element of this great prophecy (especially the answer to the disciples' question), our Lord is saying: The generation of people witnessing "the beginning of travail" (the sign) will not entirely pass away until all these things have had their fulfillment and Christ is reigning King of kings. This basic objection to this latter interpretation would seem to arise from the fear of approaching too near the territory of date-setting.

But would this be the case? Assuming for a moment the correctness of this latter view, and further assuming that World War I was the sign (we do not affirm dogmatically that it was), would there really be any warrant for date-setting? There would, to be sure, be a ringing herald of the *nearness* of the end; but would there not be too many indeterminable factors to try to set dates? We do not unduly press the point, but it does seem to us that, especially in view of the whole context, this latter interpretation of "this generation" has considerable merit and force. In fact, it appears to harmonize distinctly with our Lord's injunction to *know*, by these things, that He is *near*, but to refrain most carefully from anything approaching the setting of the exact time. We cannot but believe that He uses language without any contradiction or ambiguity, and when He tells us to know that He is near, even at the doors, He means exactly that.

As a matter of fact, being what we are, it is highly doubtful that we could be aroused to the proper attitude of eagerly expecting His return unless we had reasonable assurances He were coming in our generation. And this is surely His purpose in revealing these wonderful truths: as the terrible end-time draws nigh, He wants His people (born-again Christians) to be comforted, on the one hand, and tirelessly witnessing a consecrated witness for Him on the other. May the blessed Spirit of Truth be our infallible guide and interpreter in this, as in all other matters of the Word.

Assuming the correctness of the above conclusions, the question most naturally arises: What about World War I? Was it *the* sign of the consummation of the age? Here again we make no dogmatic statement, but, bearing in mind what we have learned about the nature of this sign, we cite a few facts for the careful consideration and prayerful meditation of the child of God.

Insofar as history records, this was the first genuine *world-wide* war. Some forty-three nations involving armies totalling 53,000,000 men were eventually involved. World-wide famines followed; also world-wide pestilences. It has been estimated that some 30,000,000 died of disease, and the influenza epidemic that followed has been called "the greatest pestilence in all history." And there have been earthquakes in divers places, so much so that it has been stated that "the earth has suffered more quakes in the last twenty years than in the rest of its existence."

And what of the budding of the fig tree (the national revival of Israel in Palestine) in relation to World War I? Many things could be pointed out here, but we mention only the very significant fact that on December 9, 1917, General Allenby captured Jerusalem without firing a shot and thus ended the twelve-hundred-year rule of the cruel Turk. Britain then took the lead in reopening Palestine as a homeland for the Jews, with the amazing result that from 50,000 in 1918 they have increased to some 2,000,000 in 1954, and Israel has *officially* existed as a sovereign nation in Palestine since May 1948! It can scarcely be gainsaid that the Lord definitely used

World War I as a means of restoring His people to their land for the role they are to play in the end-time tragedy, the latter to be followed by their leadership in the ensuing millennial kingdom of the returning Christ.

That the alarm heralding the approaching Day of the Lord should be thus associated with war (as indicated by Joel 2:1) is surely logical and understandable when considered in the light of the nature, course and end of this present evil age. One of sin's most awful fruits, and the malignant scourge of mankind, war is one of the principal ingredients in the cup of God's wrath which the Christ-rejecting world will be forced to drink in the end-time judgment. And how could the death pangs of this evil age and the birth pangs of the golden age be better pictured? And, further, does not World War II, with its greater intensity and anguish, go far toward confirming World War I as the "beginning of travail" (the "first birth pang")?

What shall we say to these things? Our Lord tells us: "When these things *begin* to come to pass, then *look up, and lift up your heads;* for your redemption draweth nigh" (Luke 21:28). *Even before* the curtain rises on the end-time tragedy, we, the Bride of Christ, will be suddenly caught up to be forever with Him. So, if the stage is about set, and the actors about ready for their end-time roles, and the first notes of the prelude already sounded, how very *soon,* may we meet our blessed Lord face to face!

Chapter XXVII

BE YE DOERS OF THE WORD

Note: See Appendix I, Definitions 23, 25, 29 and 34.

Surely as we come to the close of this survey of the fascinating Word of prophecy, "our hearts burn within us." We feel that it would be tragic neglect to conclude such a study as this without a most earnest consideration of an indispensable concluding theme: Biblical Prophecy *Applied*.

1. *"Behold, I have told you before."* With these significant words of our blessed Lord ringing in our hearts and minds, may we now, with David, the sweet Psalmist of Israel, behold how the mighty Creator makes even the heavens to confirm beautifully the sure Word of prophecy. We do not, for a moment, question that Psalm 19:1 has primary reference to the wondrous ways in which creation proclaims the glory of the Creator. But, as is so often the case, all the precious gems are not found on the surface of the Word, nor does one application exhaust its storehouse of treasures; in fact, they are truly inexhaustible. Thus, in verses 4 and 5 of this beautiful Psalm, we find a very definite hint that we are not to think of the sun in the sky, but of Him who is the Sun of Righteousness, and the Bridegroom of the Church. Therefore, we feel that we do not stray from the truth of the Word when we conclude that "the heavens declare the glory of God" in that they vividly portray the manifestation of the unspeakable glory of the returning Christ.

a. *The midnight cry.* Apart from the light of the prophetic Word, a glance at the heavens now is not reassuring. This wicked age becomes more and more enfolded in the deepening hues of its midnight gloom of evil and sin and fear. But that is when a cry is heard: "Behold the Bridegroom cometh!" Then the darkness must flee away for He is the Light. Thus is His Bride, the true Church, being awakened even in these very closing moments of her earthly sojourn, to be ready to meet her Beloved in the air and forever be with Him. And as the shadows of midnight deepen, the cry rings out more intensely, "Behold, the Bridegroom cometh!"

b. *The Morning Star.* And, as the beautiful Bright and Morning Star, He will indeed suddenly appear to snatch away His beloved Bride from this doomed earth in the quiet stillness of the pre-dawn hours. He will not then visibly come to earth, but will descend into the air and call up His own to meet Him, and to be forever with Him, even while a sin-deluded world sleeps on in gross ignorance of the awful judgments about to be loosed by a righteous God.

c. *The Sun of Righteousness*. Here indeed is it abundantly clear that "the heavens *do* declare the glory of God" in the triumphant return of His Beloved Son to this earth. First the midnight cry, then the Morning Star, then the darkest hour before dawn (the unprecedented age-ending Tribulation), and then the rising of the Sun of Righteousness, with healing in His wings, as the Lord Jesus Christ personally, literally, visibly and triumphantly returns to set up His millennial kingdom and usher in the earth's long-desired golden age.

2. "*Therefore be ye also ready*." This sums up the whole burden of prophecy's message: Our Lord says, in effect, "I have graciously condescended to unveil the future for you, so that, being forewarned, you may not be found unprepared for My return." And there would seem to be at least a three-fold application of this tremendous theme to the heart and life of the believer, and to the true Church as a whole.

a. *Be of good cheer*. "Weeping may endure for the night, but joy cometh in the morning" (Ps. 30:5); and we are also reminded that "the sufferings of this present time are not worthy to be compared with the glory which shall be revealed in us" (Rom. 8:18). An unhappy, fearful, despondent Christian is of little service to man or God and thus it is that, in the sure Word of Prophecy, our Lord has given us the perfect antidote for fear, worry and grief. He wants us to be happy, not only for our own sakes, but so that we may better witness for Him to a doomed world. To accomplish this, He does not exempt His children from the griefs and sorrows, trials and tribulations, which are the common lot of mankind in this vale of tears; but He *does* take away the sting and power of these things by assuring us there *is* a better day coming, when all tears will be wiped away and joy will eternally reign. "I *will* come again and receive you unto myself. . . .wherefore, comfort one another with these words."

b. *Be ye holy.* Shall we, especially in view of His imminent return for us, permit Satan and the wicked world to entice us into paths of sin? Shall we in any wise lock arms with a condemned, Christ-denying world, and therefore betray our lovely Lord? Shall we be found in the place of lowly compromise with a Christ-hating world, when He suddenly calls us to meet Him in the air? God forbid! Surely, surely, "He that hath this hope [of our Lord's *imminent* return] in him, purifieth himself, even as he is pure." God grant that this shall be so of His people in these tragic last days, not alone for His sake, but for the sake of poor lost sinners who will never find Christ through worldly, back-slidden Christians. And may He grant us this cleansing grace that we may not be found ashamed at His appearing, but may hear, instead, that sweetest of welcomes: "Well done, good and faithful servant; enter thou into the joy of thy Lord."

c. *Occupy till I Come.* "The time is short" (I Cor. 7:29). "The fields are white unto the harvest, and the laborers are few." The need is desperate, and the task tremendous. Judgement *is* coming; the day of God's grace *will* end; and there are yet millions upon millions eternally perishing without Him who is the Water of Life. Through the prophetic Word we have learned something of the awfulness of the doom awaiting all who die without Christ; their everlasting torment in the Lake of Fire is wholly indescribable but terribly real. Christ died for their sins; the Way is wide open to heaven; the price has been paid in full. This is the message we *must* proclaim to lost men everywhere while it is yet time. Surely the horror of a lost soul's eternal doom, and the certain imminence of the return of Christ, as so vividly and plainly seen through the Word of prophecy, cannot but arouse us, the Lord's people, out of our pitiful lethargy and indifference, and cause us to indeed be about the Master's business of winning precious souls as never before.

3. *Let us hear the conclusion of the whole matter.* For as

Solomon, the wisest of men, said centuries ago, "God shall bring every work into judgment." The day of reckoning *is* coming. God *will* yet have the final word, for we are dealing not with man's flimsy predictions and guesses but with the eternal Word of the God of the universe, who cannot lie, and whose Word can neither be changed nor gainsaid.

a. *This is the purpose that is purposed upon the whole earth.* The perfect God has a perfect plan — "He, the Lord of hosts hath purposed, and who shall disannul it? and his hand is stretched out, and who shall turn it back?" The answer to these questions is obvious: The Omnipotent One *will* perform His whole purpose earthward, as foretold in the sure Word of prophecy, exactly on time and precisely as He has said He would. Man may choose to ignore, disbelieve, or thwart God's prophetic program, even combining with Satan, His arch-enemy, in an evil all-out effort to defeat Him, but His stretched-out Hand cannot be turned back!

b. *He which testifieth these things saith, surely I come quickly!* The Lord Jesus Christ, the One who hath spoken these things, is also the One who will execute the entire earthward purposes of the Triune Godhead. He does not delegate this task to any other because there is none else worthy or able. He will return to this earthly scene *in person*, visibly, irresistibly, gloriously and triumphantly to overthrow Satan, sin and death, and eternally reign, supremely and universally, King of kings and Lord of lords!

c. *Amen. Even so, come, Lord Jesus.* A groaning creation joins His earth-weary Bride in this heart-felt plea for the altogether lovely One to rend the heavens and deliver His own from the curse and bondage of sin. And He instills this desire in our hearts as a sure token of His imminent return: soon, *perhaps very soon*, our cry shall suddenly change from "Even so, come, Lord Jesus," to the ecstatic exclamation, "Behold, the Bridegroom!"

One final word: should, perchance, this message reach one who has never trusted in Christ for his soul's salvation, we urge you with our whole heart to flee to Him from the wrath to come. "Believe on the Lord Jesus Christ, and thou shalt be saved." Do it *now*, because *now* is the accepted time. Tomorrow may be *too late!*

APPENDIX I:

DEFINITIONS

1. *Advent, First*: The literal, personal, visible and historical coming of God's Son, the Lord Jesus Christ, to this earth in the form of man to suffer and die for the sins of the world.

2. *Advent, Second*: The literal, personal, visible and future return of God's Son, the Lord Jesus Christ, to this earth in glory and great power to establish His kingdom of righteousness and peace in the world.

3. *Ages (Dispensations)*: Those successive periods of time in man's history upon this earth, during each of which the human race is tested in respect of obedience to the specifically revealed will of God. Five such ages lie in the past, we are presently in the age of grace, and the kingdom age follows; all having in common a judgment-ending because of man's failure.

4. *Antichrist, The*: Of all the deceivers coming in Christ's name down through the centuries, he is essentially *the* false messiah, properly designated the Man of Sin and the Son of Perdition. Claiming to be *the* Christ, he will, in the end of the age, appear on the worldstage and, with his satanic powers, dupe a deluded world into accepting him as the promised Messiah indeed. The personification of the Devil, he is the most notorious personage of the end-time (other than Satan himself), and is destroyed by the Lord Jesus Christ personally at His glorious return.

5. *Armageddon*: Located in Palestine, this great plain (called "the world's ideal battlefield") will be the locale of the final battle of the age, when Antichrist gathers there all the armies of his subservient world against God, God's Christ,

God's people (Israel) and God's Holy City (Jerusalem). These wicked hordes are completely overthrown by Christ triumphantly returning as King of kings and Lord of Lords.

6. *Christendom*: The whole sphere of *professing* Christianity, the *visible* church, containing all (both true and false) who *profess* to embrace the Gospel of Christ.

7. *Church, The True*: That one living organism, called the Body and Bride of Christ, made up of all who have been born again unto life eternal through personal faith in the crucified and risen Son of God.

8. *Daniel's "seventy weeks" prophecy*: A period of 490 years set apart in the counsels of God as the time during which He will finish with the sin question and bring in everlasting righteousness through the Lord Jesus Christ. At the time of Calvary 483 years had expired, and God temporarily stopped the prophetic clock, leaving seven years yet to run at the judgment-ending of this present evil age.

9. *Day of Christ*: That time when "he shall see of the travail of his soul, and shall be satisfied"; that moment of unspeakable bliss when He shall reward His raptured saints and enter the indescribable joys of "the marriage supper of the Lamb" and His Bride, beginning with and eternally following the home-call of the true Church, which is His Body.

10. *Day of the Lord*: Commencing with the unprecedented judgment-ending of this age, the "Day of the Lord" signifies the conclusion of "Man's Day" of sin and misrule on the earth, and the establishment henceforth of the supreme, universal and eternal reign of Him whose right alone it is.

11. *Eternity*: Along with the final disposition of Satan, death, sin and sinners at the Great White Throne judgment, the phenomenon we call "time" also passes out of the picture, and never ending "eternity" begins. This awesome word, beyond the comprehension of the finite mind, describes the duration of the fate of both sinner and saint: the horrible

Lake of Fire for the lost; the bliss of heaven for the saved — but both *forever*.

12. *Gentiles, Fulness of*: While both Jew and Gentile alike are brought into the true Church through personal faith in Christ (and they are there no longer distinguished as such), it nevertheless remains that He is, essentially, during this church age "taking out from among the Gentiles a people for his name." This "called-out" people is the true Church, and when the last one to be brought into the Body of Christ has been born-again, then will it be complete and then will occur the "fulness of the Gentiles," as the Bride of Christ is raptured to meet Him in the air.

13. *Gentiles, Times of*: According to Dr. Scofield's excellent definition: "The Times of the Gentiles is that long period beginning with the Babylonian captivity of Judah, under Nebuchadnezzar, and to be brought to an end by the destruction of Gentile world-power by the 'Stone cut without hands', i.e. the coming of the Lord in glory; until which time Jerusalem is politically subject to Gentile rule."

14. *Glory of Christ*: This term is synonymous with the Second Advent of Christ inasmuch as He returns to manifest His supreme glory as *the* Kings of kings and Lord of lords, to whom every knee will bow in fitting homage, and of whom every tongue will confess "He is Lord."

15. *Gog (and Magog)*: In Ezekiel 38 and 39, this has reference to the Russian dictator, his land and his allies in their great endtime invasion of Palestine, *before* the Millennium. In Revelation 20 the same term is used, but here it describes a world-wide insurrection, under Satan, against Christ and His kingdom *after* the Millennium. The same phrase is used in each case doubtless because both are viciously anti-God, and both invoke the unrestrained fury of His holy wrath.

16. *Israel*: The race descended from Abraham, Isaac and Jacob, and properly called the chosen nation because of their

centrality in God's purposes earthward. Through Israel, the Bible, God's written Word, was transmitted to and preserved for mankind; of the Jews, according to the flesh, Christ came the first time; and through Israel He will reign when He returns to establish His millennial kingdom on the earth.

17. *Judgment seat of Christ*: This has reference to the judging of the believer's works to determine the gain or loss of reward. It takes place in heaven after the Rapture, and involves only the saved, whose eternal salvation is assured by the very fact of their presence at the judgment seat of Christ, but whose rewards are to be determined according to their works on earth following their salvation.

18. *Judgment of the nations*: This takes place on the earth, at the beginning of Christ's millennial reign, and is just what the term implies: a judgment of the then-living nations to determine whether or not they shall be admitted into His kingdom. The nations are dealt with as such, and according to their attitude toward and treatment of the faithful Jewish remnant who will have, during the Tribulation, proclaimed worldwide the Gospel of the coming King.

19. *Judgment (Great White Throne)*: This is correctly called the Last Judgment; wherein all the wicked dead from Cain to the last unregenerate sinner of the Millennium will be physically resurrected to stand before the bar to hear their eternal sentence: the Lake of Fire. It fittingly takes place at the point where time merges into eternity, following the Millennium.

20. *Kingdom of heaven*: The term is self-descriptive in that it literally means the heavenly rule of Christ on earth, visibly, invincibly and *in person*. Thus, at His first advent, John the Baptist truthfully proclaimed "the kingdom is at hand" because the rightful King had come. But He was rejected and slain, so that during His present exile from earth (as it were) in this present evil age, there is no actual kingdom but instead only Christendom, the sphere of Christian profession. Apostasy

does its deadly work even in this realm where there is *professed* loyalty to Christ, and it remains for Him to return gloriously *in person* to set up His literal "kingdom of heaven" on the earth.

21. *Lake of Fire*: This awful expression is used to portray the kind of place prepared for the everlasting punishment of Satan, his angels and all of the human race that will have died without Christ. To it are they all irrevocably and eternally consigned, along with death and hell, when the great Judge pronounces the final verdict.

22. *Last days, The*: As concerning the Church, this expression has reference to the closing days of the church age, which shall become increasingly wicked and perilous, according to the Word; these are, therefore, the closing days of the true Church's sojourn on earth and the signs multiply that they are indeed already here, heralding the imminent Rapture of the Bride to meet her Lord in the air.

Otherwise, and especially as concerning Israel, "the last days" specifically refer to the seven-year judgment-ending of the present age, following the Rapture of the true Church, and immediately preceding the glorious personal return of Christ to establish His kingdom here.

23. *Midnight cry*: As the hues of this present evil age ominously darken, approaching the blackness of midnight, the Holy Spirit arouses the Bride of Christ (the true Church) with the insistent cry: "Behold, the Bridegroom cometh!" For some time now the "midnight cry" has been sounded, and it increases in volume and intensity as the hour of the Rapture draws nigh.

24. *Millennium*: The literal meaning of the word signifies its message: the thousand-year reign of Christ on earth as King of kings when He personally returns in great glory.

25. *Morning Star*: Just as midnight is followed by the rising of the beautiful morning star in the still predawn darkness, even so will He who is "the Bright and Morning Star" come

for His Bride, and call her suddenly to meet Him in the air, in fulfillment of the "midnight cry" of the Holy Spirit. And this will take place in the silent watches of the night, while the rest of the world sleeps, little aware of the terrible judgment that will befall them in that darkest hour before dawn — the great Tribulation which takes place between the coming of the "Morning Star" for His Church, and the visible manifestation of the Sun of Righteousness with healing in His wings.

26. *Palestine*: Properly called the Holy Land, Palestine is that portion of this earth which is central in God's program and purposes earthward. Given irrevocably to the Jews through Abraham, Isaac and Jacob, it embraces far more than the narrow strip presently so designated along the eastern shore of the Mediterranean. When occupied by purged and regenerated Israel in the coming days of Christ's kingdom on earth, its Holy City Jerusalem will be His world capital, and, according to the original grant from the Lord God, it will, generally speaking, take in the territory between the Mediterranean, Euphrates and Nile. Which means that the real Palestine will cover some 300,000 square miles, being twelve times larger than Great Britain and Ireland, and twenty-five times larger than the Palestine (Israel) of today.

27. *Prophecy, Biblical*: Biblical prophecy is the Holy Spirit testifying beforehand. Its *one* Subject is *Christ*. Its all-embracing divisions are: (1) The Sufferings of Christ (First Advent); and (2) The Glory of Christ to Follow (Second Advent). All other Scriptural prophecies, however vital, are subordinated to these.

28. *Prophet, False*: The sinister one, of whom all false prophets down through the ages are but foreshadows. Basically a prophet is one who speaks forth to men a message from God; this goes far to explain the relation, in the end-time, of *the* False Prophet to *the* Antichrist. The latter claims to be God manifested in the flesh, and the False Prophet seems to be

his chief spokesman during their brief but terrible rule in the Tribulation period. It might be otherwise stated that the False Prophet will, in a sense, be the religious counterpart of the political Antichrist, the two being essentially one in their personification of Satan, their master, and both finding themselves cast alive into the Lake of Fire at Christ's return.

29. *Rapture, The*: The coming of the Lord Jesus Christ, the Bridegroom, for His Bride, the true Church, *before* the age-ending Tribulation befalls this doomed world. In a moment of time, all living believers will suddenly be caught up at His call, together with the then-resurrected dead in Christ, to meet Him in the air and to be forever with Him.

30. *Resurrection, First*: Guaranteed by Christ's victory over the grave, physical resurrection unto life is assured all the saved at His return. All the dead in Christ (both O.T. and N.T. saints) will be so raised when He comes for the Church, and the first resurrection will be completed when He raises the martyred Tribulation Saints upon His visible return at the close of that awful judgment period.

31. *Resurrection, Second*: This term is best defined by contrast: whereas the first resurrection is of the redeemed, *before* the Millennium and unto life eternal, the second is of the unsaved, *after* the Millennium and unto the eternal Lake of Fire (the second death). The only point of similarity is that each is a literal, physical resurrection.

32. *Satan*: Originally Lucifer (Son of the Morning), this mighty one appears to have been at the top of the created order before sin was born in his heart through pride and rebellion against his Maker, causing his fall from heaven and his transformation into Satan, the source of sin and arch-enemy of God and man. His doom was sealed when Christ overcame his most powerful weapon, death; and his eternal fate will be realized when Christ binds him at His glorious return and casts him into the Lake of Fire at the close of the Millennium.

33. *Sufferings of Christ*: This phrase is synonymous with the First Advent, when the Lamb of God came to suffer and die for the sins of the world.

34. *Sun of Righteousness*: This beautiful expression graphically depicts the Second Coming of Christ in power and great glory, to end man's day of the darkness of sin, and to usher in the Lord's day of light, righteousness and peace — the "golden age."

35. *Tribulation, The*: The term fittingly describes the unprecedented age-ending judgments from an aroused and holy God, which will befall this wicked world after the Rapture of the true Church, and which will immediately precede the glorious return of Christ to earth in person. The Tribulation corresponds to the seventieth week (seven years) of Daniel's great time-prophecy, which will conclude God's righteous program earthward; and the last three and one-half years of these seven years are properly designated the *Great* Tribulation because of the awful intensity of anguish upon earth in the midst of God's outpoured wrath.

APPENDIX II:

A KEY-OUTLINE TO MATTHEW 24 AND 25

1. The Occasion and the Disciples' Questions: 24:1-3.
2. Christ's Warning Against Deception: 24:4, 5.
3. The Course of This Present Age in Summary: 24:6.
4. The Beginning of Travail: The Sign of the Consummation of the Age: 24:7, 8.
5. A Description of the Seven-year Tribulation with Particular Emphasis on the First three and one-half Years: 24:9-14
6. Added Details Concerning the Seven-year Age-ending Tribulation with Particular Emphasis on the Last three and one-half Years (The *Great* Tribulation): 24:15-26.
7. The Glorious Return to Earth of Christ, the King of kings, At End and Climax of the Great Tribulation: 24:27-30.
8. The Completion by Christ of Israel's Final Regathering to Her Land: 24:31.
9. The Certainty and Force of These Signs: 24:32-35.
10. Christ's Solemn Warnings Against Date-Setting: 24:36.
11. Urgent Warning and Exhortations in View of the Imminent Return of Christ to Earth: 24:37-25:30.
12. Christ's Judgment of the Nations at His Return to Establish His Kingdom on Earth: 25:31-46.

APPENDIX III:

A KEY-OUTLINE TO REVELATION
KEY-VERSE: REV. 1:19

I. "The things which thou hast seen": The Glorified Christ and His Commission to John (Chapter 1).
II. "The things which are": The Pre-Written History of the Church Age (Chapters 2 and 3).
III. "The things which shall be hereafter": Chapters 4-22:
   1. The Rapture of the Church Signified: 4:1, 2.
   2. Heavenly Scenes Following the Rapture of the Church and Preceding the Tribulation: 4:2-5:14.
   3. The Seven-year Tribulation: The Wrath of the King: 6-19:6.
   4. The Marriage Supper of the Lamb and His Bride (the Raptured Church) in Heaven (During the Tribulation on Earth): 19:7-10.
   5. The Glorious and Triumphant Return to Earth of the King of kings *with* His Saints (the Redeemed) at the Close of the Tribulation: 19:11-16.
   6. The Utter Defeat of Antichrist and His Armies by the Triumphantly Returning King of kings: 19:17-21.
   7. The Binding of Satan (the Deceiver of the Nations), and the Glorious Thousand-year Reign of Christ on Earth: 20:1-6.
   8. Satan's Brief Release, Final Rebellion and Eternal Doom: 20:7-10.

9. The Final Judgment (the Great White Throne), and Eternal Doom of the Wicked Dead: 20:11-15.
10. The New Heaven and New Earth — Eternity: 21, 22.

APPENDIX IV:

THE VITAL RELATION OF THE SECOND COMING TO OTHER DOCTRINES OF THE SCRIPTURES

1. Antichrist: II Thess. 2:8.
2. Apostasy: II Pet. 2:1.
3. Ascension: Acts 1:11.
4. Assurance: II Tim. 1:12 and Heb. 6:11.
5. Body: Rom. 8:23-25; Phil. 3:21; I John 3:2, 3.
6. Crucifixion: Zech. 12:10.
7. Death: I Cor. 15:51-57.
8. Deliverance of Creation: Rom. 8:19-23.
9. Glory: II Thess. 1:10.
10. Grace: Eph. 2:4-9.
11. Heaven: John 14:1-3.
12. Holiness: I John 3:2, 3.
13. Hope: Titus 2:13-15.
14. Inheritance: I Pet. 1:3-5.
15. Judgment: Acts 17:31.
16. Kingdom: Dan. 7:13, 14.
17. Lord's Day: Heb. 10:25.
18. Lord's Supper: I Cor. 11:23-26.
19. Millennium: Rev. 19:11-20:6.
20. Patience: James 5:7, 8.
21. Peace: Is. 2:2-4; Is. 9:6, 7.
22. Prayer: Matt. 6:9, 10.
23. Punishment: II Thess. 1:7-10.
24. Repentance: I Thess. 1:9, 10.
25. Resurrection: Acts 2:25-31.

26. Rewards: Rev. 22:12.
27. Salvation: I Thess. 1:9, 10.
28. Satan: Rev. 20:1-10.
29. Security: Jude 24, 25.
30. Service: Matt. 24:46.
31. Sin: I Cor. 15:24-26, 56.
32. Sonship: I John 3:2.
33. Stewardship: Rom. 14:11, 12.
34. Suffering: Rom. 8:18.
35. Vengeance: II Thess. 1:7, 8.